YOUR DAYS,

HERBERT

3-Minute Heydays *LAW!*

Ed Hayes

Pineapple Press, Inc.
Sarasota, Florida

With exuberant thanks to Mom and Dad, who gave me my first big break in life; to Tom and Jim, who let me be on the team; and to Betty Ann, for saying yes.

Also by Ed Hayes
The Day of the Game
a novel
The Florida One-Day Trip Book
with Betty Ann Weber
Best of Heydays

Inquiries should be addressed to:

Pineapple Press, Inc.
P.O. Box 3889
Sarasota, Florida 34230

www.pineapplepress.com

Library of Congress Cataloging-in-Publication Data

Hayes, Edward, 1924–
   Three-minute heydays / by Ed Hayes.— 1st ed.
      p. cm.
   ISBN 1-56164-297-5 (alk. paper)
   I. Title.
   PN4874.H357A25 2004
   814'.54—dc22

                                                    2003022061

First Edition
10 9 8 7 6 5 4 3 2 1

Design by Shé Heaton
Printed in the United States of America

Contents

Called 59

THE SPORTS BEAT: ALL PLAY AND NO WORK

'Tis the Season 83

CHRISTMAS: AND ALL THROUGH THE CALENDAR

We Do! We Do!   131

ALL IS WELL: SKIPPING ALONG TO OUR VOWS

My Greatest Generation   155

MUGGED AND HUGGED: WELCOME ABOARD, BOOMERS

Introduction

Reading Time: 3 Minutes

More or less.

When I was a young fellow devouring all those fantastic magazines on the newsstands, one of my favorites was *Liberty*. Actually, *Colliers* prevailed as my all-time top periodical, but always I was intrigued by the "reading time" labels the *Liberty* editors posted on each short story and article. Exactly why or when the practice started or discontinued, I can't say. That stuff is beside the point anyway.

Which brings us up to 1989—the year Stephen McKenney Steck, president of WMFE-TV/FM in Orlando, invited me to join his roster of Public Radio essayists; with the suggestion I employ a format much in the same length, tune, and fiber of *Heydays,* my weekly 500-word column in the *Orlando Sentinel*. In short, I'd be taking a look around at the world of today and yesterday, and speaking to a general audience from the perch of a retired individual—that is, someone who is retired from the general work force and who happens to be drawing Social Security.

As for the frequency of my appearances on the air, Dave Pignanelli, then the station's vice president of programming, left it up to me—weekly, every other week, monthly, whatever appealed to me. I picked weekly. The way I figure, if you're going to do something, *do* it. Besides, after all these years, I've become fond of deadlines. There's something—well, let's see, how do I put this, something *everlasting* about deadlines. They're like little flags up ahead on the track, letting you know that somebody's wait-

1

ing for you, that you're still important.

And so each week I'm entrusted with three minutes of Central Florida's Public Air—a neat little slot because that's about the average time it takes to read my column. For several obvious reasons, then, I decided to call the broadcast series *3-Minute Heydays,* and it's the title I've chosen to carry this book, a collection of hand-picked columns from among those which have appeared in the *Sentinel* over the last decade.

Take note, though, that the clinching vote on the issue of a title was cast by David Cussen, publisher of Pineapple Press. He was taken by it, so that was that.

My guess is that either Pineapple Press or I will be hearing from readers who claim they can breeze through any given entry in, say, two minutes or less. Maybe in even *one* minute.

Fine. Speed readers are as welcome as anyone. Mostly what we're interested in here is that the pieces be *read,* and taken to heart. Sorry, no prizes for swiftness.

And so now, before withdrawing and turning this book over to you, I must squeeze in thanks to Betty Ann Weber, my wife and in-house editor, who sees to it that my work is successfully imported into the newspaper's database downtown.

And to Loraine O'Connell, the first editor at the paper each week to get her hands on my efforts, and to her office mate Eleanor Trouse for years of allegiant technical support.

Plus a snappy salute to Harry A. Haines, the first person to pay me for something I wrote, while he was still running things at the *Courier News* in Blytheville, Arkansas.

OK, your three minutes are up. Bon voyage.

Ed Hayes
Orlando
Spring, 2004

In the Beginning

On the Ninth Day of July

My mom gave birth to a bawling baby boy on a Wednesday evening in St. Louis on the ninth day of July in 1924. Although I can't personally vouch for this, you can bet the city was hotter'n a firecracker that year, not unlike most every July before and after. Sure, one can say that this historic event was a labor of love for my mom, but, pragmatically, such frothy thoughts did little to lessen the pangs and the feverish temperature in that airless second-story flat.

When the midwife, the indispensable Mrs. Amick, announced that I was a boy—and a hairy one at that—my long-legged Uncle Fred, who lived across the alley with my widowed grandma, went galloping through the neighborhood strewing the good news to interested parties.

They'd expected a girl, but Anna, his oldest sister, had just brought a second son into the world. And the trumpets blared and the rockets flared. Or maybe that was only a dream. My first. Hello, world.

Ours was an *Our Town* sort of neighborhood, that's it, shoulder-to-shoulder bungalows and two-story flats separated only by walkways and low wire fences for the most part. Window screens and screen doors held the flies and summer critters at bay, and opened the houses to the first available breeze—and threw privacy right out the window.

Children in almost every house. And now another mouth for my dad to feed.

Oh, yes, you could hear them all in the good ole summertime, life athrob, indoors, in the backyards, the alleys and streets, Tom, Jim, Jack, Bobby, Ollie, Marjorie, Lawrence, Dorothy, Marion, Boots, Betty. They were all there, Richard, Manette, Cyril, Olive, Calvin, Frances and Francis, Carl, Ralph, Raymond, Rudy, Bernice, Thelma, Willie, Bill, and Gil—their mamas and daddies calling them to task, to supper, and calling one to the other.

Lord, we were such little creatures at one time, seen and heard, skipping and laughing, shooting marbles, swinging bats, kicking and screaming, jumping rope, cranking ice-cream makers on back porches, playing step ball and mumblety-peg, and tossing firecrackers.

If I'd arrived in this world a few days prematurely, I might've been a Yankee Doodle Dandy, born on the fourth of July—the night the neighbors always sat on the lawns to watch the fireworks sponsored by the local hardware store.

So where have those boys and girls been all this time? Are they still with us? Still out there somewhere, posing as grandpas and grandmas?

Everybody knows that time is faster than the speed of light, but there was one evening not so very long ago when time stood stock still, when it took my mom in its arms.

Would that upstairs bedroom never cool off? The discomfort and pain never stop? And then, whew, the clock was ticking again. I was born.

They were solid, honest, hard-working people living in our neighborhood.

Hope I didn't keep anyone awake that night.

Oh, You Beautiful Baby

I must've been a beautiful baby. You know why? 'Cause, baby, look at me now.

OK, only kidding around. The foregoing words are a slight switcheroo of the old popular song.

Don't ask me for reasons, but this standard number—"You Must've Been a Beautiful Baby," words and music by Johnny Mercer and Harry Warren—has been bounding about in my head for several days now.

Conceivably the process could be connected to the afternoon last week when my wife and I went shopping for baby diapers. As I explained to the store cashier who sized me up with a conspicuously leery eye, we were buying the sizable package of diapers as a donation to our church's continuing agenda of helping out young, needy families.

When I asked the clerk if perchance safety pins were included in the package she merely shook her head slightly and smiled—suspiciously. I took this response to mean that when it comes to "changing" babies nowadays, pins are passé. Hope I got that right.

As for myself being a beautiful baby, who knows, maybe I really *was*. Aren't all babies? At least when they recoup from the initial shock of opening their eyes to this world?

I put the question to my wise older brother. Since all my baby pictures apparently have been burned, he's my only kinsman today who'd know what I looked like back then. He said he obscurely recalls our mom parading me up and down the sidewalks in a flashy, covered, four-wheeled buggy, and stopping every so often to accommodate "the ladies" who bent down to peer into the carriage.

"Oh, what a beautiful baby." Anyway, that's what *he* said.

"My, what a beautiful little boy." He claims he even remembers one woman leaning over and bubbling, "Ah, what a beautiful little girl."

At all counts, I ponder about how my mom and dad genuinely felt when they beheld me for the first time on that hot Wednesday in July of '24—other than the obvious fact that I was a handsome tyke, of course. What did they perceive about my destiny, or about their own chances of personal fulfillment as individuals and as a man and a woman in love who'd locked hands and decided to raise a family?

All right, how about the feelings and intentions of the unknown progenitors to whom my wife and I bequeathed those recently purchased disposable diapers? I pray the parents aren't overpowered by the outlook of bringing another little soul into a universe on tenterhooks.

Has there *ever* been a model time to beget offspring, an era devoid of war or pestilence or treachery or—well, how about the Great Depression? A raft of kids made it through OK, born in the '20s, nurtured in the topsy-turvy '30s, rich kids without knowing it, each doing his or her own part with all our hearts, scrambling to circumvent the capitulation of civilization.

And we were all beautiful babies too, I bet.

Hear, Hear the Whistler

I know exactly where I was when it happened the first time. My exact age is less clear. Nine, maybe ten, somewhere in that grand old neighborhood.

We lived about three and a half blocks from school, my destination that morning, and I was roughly halfway there. Tightening my lips, fixing my tongue just so, I inhaled deeply, then blew for all I was worth. It was a facial maneuver I'd been practicing for months without any compelling results.

On this day, lo and behold, out came a harsh, brash, somewhat abrasive sound, but definitely definable as a whistle, the type referred to in another time as a newsboy's whistle. Not to put too fine a point to this, but it differs radically from the more common, melodious whistle. That is, the kind created by forming a little "o" on one's pursed lips, then blowing through it. The newsboy's is more difficult. Matter of fact, some practitioners require two fingers in the mouth to help pull it off.

At all counts, please try to imagine my incredulity and exhilaration. There I am, a little kid walking up the sidewalk alone, and without the aid of any fingers and after months of intermittent trials, an astounding sound suddenly blasts from inside me.

Smile if you want, chuckle or laugh, but it was the pinnacle of wonder. Actually, it frightened me some. I looked all around. There were no other boys or girls up ahead or behind. I tried it again. It worked. Louder and clearer. So it wasn't a fluke. And in the distance a dog answered. What power.

Not only was the whistle an invisible attention-getting tool, engineered to carry great distances, I also knew it to be employed by big league infielders to keep their team-mates alert. Definitely a masculine thing.

I chuckled to myself, trying to picture a girl walking up the street whistling in this fashion. I sooner would've expected to hear one of them utter a cuss word. Which was unthinkable.

At my school desk I practiced a few soundless whistles, fearing I might lose my touch, but it's like blowing your nose. Once you get the hang of it, you never forget.

Quietly I marvel today at how little it took for me at the time to shiver with the intoxication of attainment. And I ponder the dreams and tests and triumphs that propel today's boys and girls. It can't be easy, born under the sign of overkill.

When I was a small feller, everything seemed within reach. Now, every day is an unfinished race.

How easy it must be to get caught up in a world where so much has to be swifter and louder, a nonstop world of television and computer images and challenges. I hope children find time to stop and sniff, and whistle, that their impossible dreams don't wear out long before their time.

What a dismal eventuality it'd be for me right now, at my age, to run out of expectations.

Beware: Grand Opening

Come with me now as I stride down the corridor of my old high school and stop smugly in front of my locker.

Oh, yes, having one's own locker was one of the smug splendors of advancing to this level of education.

Think of it. For the first time in my life, here was the capability of being able to keep something of my own under lock and key. Only someone living with two brothers—or under some similar sibling arrangement—in pinched quarters, can relish this.

And now as I stand here digging into my pocket for my own private locker key, I again feel like a hotshot executive. Not a shabby way, as we used to say, to start a school day.

Alas, some boards of education today in my geographic subdivision of the world are eliminating lockers altogether. That's right. Or excluding them from their budgets for costly school construction, renovation, and maintenance. Too often, proclaim the overseers of the superfluous, lockers are utilized to stash drugs and weapons—unthinkable implements during my youthful interlude—and serve as hangouts for students.

Aw, don't young people always manage to find *some* place to hang out?

Speaking of hanging out, I lived in a colder climate back then, and since we no longer had access to the old grammar school cloakroom, or wrap room, we needed space to store our jackets and coats and stuff—and paste our pinups.

In my life, at least, the locker represented the last stronghold of privacy. Of course, I'd soon be a *private* in the U.S. Army, but that was the classic misnomer of all time—as Irving Berlin once melodiously pointed out.

The majority of us marry and rear families. That fact of life, coupled with the electronic revolution, dwarfs our private realm by the hour. On the surface it seems lamentable that the storied sanctuaries of the young might be deleted, and yet, mind you, my intent is not to spar with school boards. They know more about the budgets and wards of their dominion than I. Actually, I *salute* all these valiant men and women for digging in and tackling vital, often thankless assignments.

Besides, to be downright forthright about it, some of those old school lockers also rated as prime examples of society's less fragrant commodities. As an example, the many boys and girls who carried their lunches to school stored them in their lockers. Singularly offensive was the pastrami or sardine sandwich, or the boiled egg—after lodging on a stifling shelf with a ripening banana for four hours. Blended with the smell of unwashed gym shorts, sneakers, and unmentionables, there existed a potentially explosive atmosphere.

In any event, I thank you, the reader, for accompanying me this far on the walk down the nostalgic school corridor, but you may now go about your own business.

Or at least step back.

I'm about to open that old locker of mine.

Back Home on the War Front

Things don't look so hot on the war front.
And by the time this newspaper hits the street, the picture,
God forbid, might look considerably more odious.

Oh, so true.

But then again, there's the clear possibility that the
state of this spectacular old world of ours will look more
promising than a garden of rosebuds.

If I can stand eyewitness to anything at all after thrash-
ing about for three-quarters of a century on this Earth, it's
this: You never know. Or as the Good Book prophesies:
"For you shall hear of wars and rumors of wars."

I heard. In fact, I went off to one of 'em to see what it
was all about.

It wasn't nice.

Oh, sure, I ought to have known what to expect. I'd
seen the motion pictures, and read the books, and absorbed
the agonies and deprivations, but you really don't know
until you've walked onto the stage.

That's right. Sit through all the gory Oscar-nominated
movies and you still don't know the smell of it. Not until
you look at yourself in the mirror and check out the
stranger in the itchy uniform, and then try not to laugh or
to bawl. Not until you realize you can't turn your new suit
of clothes back to the clerk behind the counter in exchange
for your old civilian threads. Not until *you* hop aboard a
boat and paddle across an ocean, set foot in a quaint land,
and await the first shot.

Actually, I didn't just pick up one day and head out.

Like millions of other fellows not old enough to vote, I
was drafted into Uncle Sam's army, heralded as the best-
equipped, best-trained fighting machine of all time.

I guess my older brother wasn't too swayed by all that hoopla. The first of our clan to march off—not counting the old story-spinning uncles of World War I—he joined the navy. And then one night we were down at my aunt's house for his farewell party, and everybody was having a merry time until—until it came time for my brother to pick up his toilet kit and wave goodbye to all.

And, oh, brother, my mom did cry. I'd not heard the like of it. I wish the old men who started the war could've heard the downpour.

Late that night after walking home, we found my big brother in bed, trying to hold back *his* tears. Alas, the navy had sent him back, postponing his departure for a fortnight. My brother felt abandoned, mortified, how could he face everybody? But Mom sat on the edge of his bed in the dark and they talked, and somehow time did move along and then he was gone again, only this time it seemed easier.

I'm not saying it was a happy Mother's Day or anything like that for her. She still had two more sons to send off.

I don't think any mom ever cries herself out.

May all the wars turn out to be rumors.

Gone with the Draft

*D*raft.

Now *there* was a word for us young fellows to joke around with after it burst from newspapers and radios and into our lives. Some of the older, wiser guys came up with bad gags about draft *beer,* stuff like that. But we knew what the newspapers were talking about all right—compulsory service in the armed forces. Conscription was another word for it. However, it's unlikely that many lads in my circle were as familiar with the synonym, even though it'd been inscribed in the *Congressional Record* way back in 1792.

And now, today, in the gloom of global unrest, some congressmen are once more talking draft, fostering mandatory military tooling for our young and able-bodied.

This time around, women would not be exempt.

I was a mere, unkissed, sweet sixteen when the military draft launched in 1940, and there was substantial reason to doubt that it'd ever collar me. Uncle Sam wanted the old guys, twenty-one to thirty-five. Even so, the system offered abounding adventurous possibilities, and we were not at war—yet.

Two fleeting years later they lowered the boom. The age for draftees plunged to eighteen. Suddenly, I took my own lot more seriously.

Conscription was in full swing, and the war was going full speed. Somebody would be hurt; somebody would die. That's it. But I couldn't afford to invest all my thoughts and emotions in anything so harshly inescapable or predetermined.

In a roundabout way, I looked forward to getting yanked from my civilian job, a decent occupation, though one I'd never bragged about. This particular firm had furnished respectable incomes in hard times for a batch of men and women in our clan, several of whom had engaged in string pulling to get my name on the payroll. Each passing day dimmed my vision of ever garnering the mettle to walk off the job and announce that henceforth I'd be devoting all my moments to writing beautiful stories.

I put in military time myself for what I thought was the right reason and was summarily stunned when so many young Americans burned their draft cards in 1965. They were appallingly wayward, I felt, but with each passing year I've become more compassionate. I don't have a direct line to the youths of today as to how they feel about the likelihood of being drafted.

And so there I stood, army-bound on that April morn in '43, toilet kit in hand, in our kitchen, saying goodbye, grinning from ear to ear untruthfully, feeling wretched, not knowing where I'd land or if ever I'd be back.

My older brother was already in the navy, but that wasn't going to make life easier for anybody in that house. My kid brother, my steadfast sidekick, would come in from high school baseball practice late that afternoon, and Mom'd return from a trip to the grocery store, and Dad'd arrive home from work, and there'd be another empty chair at the supper table that night.

Who Goes There?

$\mathcal{S}ilence\ marched\ in\ step\ with\ me,\ down$ along the dim streets and around the footpaths between rows of sleeping, two-story barracks. Well past twelve. On a moonless night.

Then, from out of the midnight blue: strewn echoes of a human voice.

I halted in my tracks. My heart speeded up. All at once the rifle riding my shoulder felt like a telephone pole. Dead ahead, a hundred yards distant, a lone figure materialized from the billowing veils.

My prayer, that the sojourner would take either a right or a left into the crossing street and on out of my jurisdiction, was turned down. On the obscure figure came, up the middle of the street of Company C.

"Halt! Who goes there?"

Those were the sharp-edged words, according to the manual, I was expected to yell commandingly into the night—and did not. I was still a teenager, remember, only a month in the army, but sage enough to speculate that the encroaching stranger was no mortal enemy of the United States.

Question: If he *was* a German or Japanese spy, shouldn't he be skulking from shadow to shadow, rather than jabbering to himself, and, as now, of all things, singing drunkenly?

Of course none of that was mine to judge. My charge: challenge the intruder for breaking curfew, then summon the corporal of the guard for the orderly wrap-up.

"Corporal of the guard! Post number three!"

No, I couldn't do it, simply couldn't see myself wailing those words to the nocturnal heavens. And thereby bringing help on the run, and waking up the nearby slumbering soldiers. What would it prove, that we had just another lonely GI on our hands, with one too many under his belt and who couldn't find his bunk?

Slyly I slipped between two buildings and wrapped myself in a shadow until my adversary staggered past.

Today, sixty years later, President Bush makes a pitch for defense funds to dismantle terrorist organizations and beef up our armed services for war. What if it comes to pass that there aren't enough bodies to fill the ranks? Will another Selective Service Act, like the one that pegged me in 1943, be enacted? As I mull these ponderous matters, my mind swirls back to the above World War II incident.

Suddenly, for the first time, I wonder: How did the wayward soldier, at that hour, manage to stumble into my area deep in the sprawling camp without challenge? I smile. Obviously the camp had been staffed that night with meek guards, as callow and confused as I. We were only boys, for goodness sakes, who woke up one day in uniform. But the country needed us, and we soon got the hang of it, and we KO'd two of time's mightiest war machines.

The enemy swaggered down our street, you see, and we young lions girded our loins, and with rifles cocked we leapt from the shadows, demanding: "Halt! Hold it right there, buster!"

Going Home Again

My plan was to sit in the back seat and have the taxi driver hustle around to open the door for me. Just to see how it felt to be treated like a gentleman again. I couldn't do it. Eagerly I jacked the door open and tossed my duffel bag out on the sidewalk in front of our family's first-floor flat.

Before climbing the two short flights to our front porch, I peered down toward my aunt's house at the other end of the block, and saw her, and my mom, on the sidewalk. They were looking up this way, trying to make out if it was really the soldier come home. Then they began waving and plodding up the familiar tree-lined hill. We met halfway, and there prevailed abundant kissing and hugging, crying and laughing—as any number of neighbors could testify.

A few hours later I was at the front door waiting for my dad to come home from work, the way I used to wait as a little boy.

"He looks different," said my smiling, moist-eyed dad to my mom.

And why not? I'd played a bit part in the war, but I was also twenty-one and that meant I'd come home a man.

But the family portrait wasn't complete yet—my older brother and the younger one were still in the navy and coast guard, respectively—our house stayed lighted up longer than usual that night in celebration.

It was the night I went in to use the bathroom and take a bath in *privacy* for the first time in two years. The date: January 22, 1946.

Several days ago, I had occasion to hunt through the repository of my personal papers. And for the first time in a long time came across my Army of the United States Honorable Discharge. Dated: 22 January 1946.

And my life did flash before my eyes.

Once more I was part of it, a bunch of us lucky guys arriving from around the country, the world, into the separation center. Mission: conversion back into civilians. It took awhile for this to sink in. I was fresh off the Liberty ship from Wakayama, and the long train haul from Seattle, and back at Jefferson Barracks, Missouri, where the expedition had started.

I beheld the discharge in my hands the other day, and I was riding home in the cab again, and embracing my folks, and filling my soul with all the sights and smells of home, and sleeping like a babe in my own bed.

In all likelihood they weren't my most critical hours ever, and yet, for a few grand moments I had the privilege of looking in on one sweet day in my life, as Emily did in Thornton Wilder's *Our Town*.

What's the use of tromping through it all, serving your country honorably, or in living to a certain ripe age, if you can't tap into certain random days and relive them with pride and comfort and joy?

Erin Blows Into Town

All was serene outside our house. Nothing was stirring. Not even a leaf.

How difficult it was to comprehend that the headwinds of a hurricane were gyrating only a hundred miles away, taking a deep breath and getting ready to blow point-blank at Vero Beach—and all points west across the Florida peninsula.

Later that night, the man next door came hammering at the door, inquiring if we needed assistance in battening down the hatches. With thanks most profuse we assured him we were OK, and then he was off down the road, selflessly, robustly, to ask the same question of other neighbors. But he'd be back at our door in the morning, grinning in his glistening wet, yellow poncho, with a propane stove and radio in hand to help us weather the tempest.

Who said the Good Samaritan was dead?

Anyway, it was toward three o'clock that morning, when lying awake in bed, I heard the arrival of the spooky winds stirring and shaking the high treetops around us. The sopping, gnarly fingers of my first hurricane had reached us.

A couple of hours later, my wife returned to bed after meandering through the house and shook me awake to share the news that the electric power in the house had just been KO'd. Well, it was all right, I could understand her wanting company at that time.

And for a melancholy moment I suddenly thought of my mom, gone these last thirty years now, and how grateful I was that she didn't have to live through this blustery night with us. Typically a strong presence in the house, she disconnected when fierce summer storms came bashing down on our little house. Especially when Dad was away at work. Tearful and trembling, she'd gather her three little sons unto her at the kitchen sink, and burn palms that had been blessed at the church on Palm Sunday morning. And lead us in a litany of wailing supplications that the bouncing thunder would not pulverize our house or the lightning strike us dead.

It's not that I didn't believe in the efficacy of prayer. But back in those tremulous days, I was actually more fearful that the wild flames of those burning palms in Mom's quavering hands would ignite the window curtains over the sink and burn the house down.

Obviously we brothers were always overjoyed when our dad, the smiling Irishman, came home. Sure'n it's no stretch of the truth, either, to say that I felt the protective presence of my dad the other night, when a hurricane, ironically named *Erin,* came flying through.

I do wish my dad truly had been here. Years ago when still living with my parents in St. Louis and looking for a newspaper job, I told my him that maybe one day soon we'd all be moving to Florida. Oh, it's doubtful that any prospect could've enthralled him more—except, perhaps, a visit back to his native land.

Sad to say, he never made the trip to either place.

My Tree

I've planted a tree.

Granted, it's not much. Glance at it, and you'll see it's just a skinny little thing.

But it's imbedded in the earth, and I put it there, and it's taken firm hold, as if it's at home there, and sprouting ever so nicely. Fresh, healthy, emerald leaves that weren't in existence last year, have come into our universe.

The rich conglomerate world of horticulture has opened a branch in my backyard. Master gardeners around town would surely suppress grins and chuckles over my unrestrained language and hyperbolic enthusiasm, but it's OK. See, never before have I planted anything of this grandeur.

In the past, and a quite distant past at that, my most ambitious sowing was a tomato crop. Even then it was at the direction of my wasting mom, whose crippling arthritis ultimately kept her out of the fruit, flower, and vegetable furrows forever. 'Twas a bleak day indeed when she could no longer plant anything. Although we were big-city folks, she and my Uncle Fred down the street had something perpetually colorful or salubrious surfacing in their long, narrow, fenced yards.

From my boyhood I remember in particular the endless yield of the plumpest, best-tasting tomatoes imaginable, and zesty, crunchy radishes galore.

Oddly, although my uncle never planted a tree in his own yard, he and Aunt Adeline, in the last decade of his life, moved from St. Louis into the country near Hermann, Missouri, where they helped their daughter and son-in-law and their burgeoning family cultivate a sprawling Christmas tree farm.

Myself, well, I never thought about planting a tree until about three months ago. My wife and I were out on an early morning walk when a neighbor sprang out at us from the dense foliage at the front of his home. After a warm salutation, he divulged that he'd been nursing a collection of pink-leafed tabebuia saplings, and expressed the desire that we might take one off his hands, and set it out on our estate.

My wife looked at me. The concept held instant appeal.

Unhesitatingly I said, "Yes," as if I'd been waiting a long time for someone to ask.

Several days ago, I stepped over to the railing of our sun deck with one of my in-laws and motioned proudly toward my tree.

"Who planted it for you?" he said. "Your lawn man?" It was probably the best thing he could've said to me. No, I'd dug the hole, driven the stake, and secured the tree myself.

Before pulling up a chair to write this piece today, I went down in the yard to measure my tabebuia. I've been nourishing it with plenty of water, and it's now doubled in size to four feet.

"I hope you'll be able to stand in the shade of this tree one day." Touching words from my wife.

It's only a little thing. I know that. But it has my name on it.

World Cup Stuff

After pushing through the cemetery's tall, squealing iron turnstile, visitors had the option of following the ascending trail to the right, or a similar path to the left. During the day, especially Sunday afternoons, a steady flow of folks could be seen wending to the right toward the endless acres of tombstones, old and new, small and ornate. They were older visitors mostly, armed with sprinkler cans, garden tools, and flowers to tidy up the graves of loved ones.

As a boy I never thought much about that portion of the cemetery, or the people trudging that hill. Back on this other half, you see, lay this glorious, practically treeless prairie of weeds and wild grass, far as the nude eye could measure. In effect, our private playground.

The bulk of our after-school sporting adventures took place on empty lots, and in the streets and alleys, but frequently on weekends and during the long days of summer we'd hike to the cemetery. No matter how often we invaded, or how many athletic fields we carved there, the owners never objected. Actually, it was good PR for them. Sooner or later, in all likelihood, they figured we'd end up as their paying customers.

Be that as it may or may not be, this was the spread on which I learned the joys of playing soccer. And this was the scene back to which my memory carried me when I learned that Orlando would be a host city for World Cup soccer games.

Think of it. Action of global significance enacted on a stage less than a ten-minute drive from home.

Why, if I open my windows I might even catch the roar of a crowd with an Irish brogue.

That is, if supporters of Ireland's national team have anything to whoop about. I bumped into an Irish priest downtown the other day, and wearin' a worried look he was.

Said he, "This is not the strongest Irish team of recent years."

Also, he was stewing about the lads—more accustomed to foul weather—having to compete under a subtropical sun. He's not the first to whimper about this, nor is it likely he'll be the last. And they all make good points.

Some of the best soccer I ever saw was played in cold weather by sweater-wearing boys with runny noses. Ah, indeed we did have some grand games up there on that cemetery slab. World Cup stuff. Well, weren't our parents or grandparents from Croatia, Bohemia, Germany, Italy, and Ireland?

My Irish dad got a kick out of soccer, and were he alive and able-bodied, I'd make sure he got to see Ireland's game in the Florida Citrus Bowl. Even if it'd take my monthly Social Security check to pull it off.

But he's not. He's buried next to my mom in that cemetery in the old neighborhood, within a boot and a holler from the field where we young ones played and laughed and ran and ran.

Until darkness called us home.

There Goes the Neighborhood

Watch Out: Don't Let the Bugbears Bite

The Infamous Buss

Days later, when good little boys went back to being rapscallions, you could still see evidence of Christmas gifts at school and around the neighborhood.

A shiny new pair of roller skates in action, for example.

In my place of birth in the Midwest, snow or ice wasn't a guaranteed condition in late December, so a boy or girl would be more apt to wind up with roller skates, something to be utilized year-round, rather than ice skates. Or spiffy snowshoes.

Santa Claus was more sensible during that era—especially after those intangible terrorists struck the New York Stock Exchange on October 29, 1929. Inevitably, in roller hockey games out on our brick street, one kid might be flashing a new, honest-to-goodness, St. Louis Flyers hockey stick, while the rest of us made do with our mop and broom sticks.

You could also count on several glossy-eyed students returning to class from the long holiday with new Eversharp writing implements—or reasonable facsimiles—clasped to shirts and middy blouses like distinguished badges. Twist the top of one and presto! A tip of lead protruded from the cylinder. I'd never seen anything like it. The cheaper copies of these mechanisms performed poorly.

After a while, the only way to keep the lead from slipping out of my yellow Eversharp look-alike was to hold the instrument upside down.

New fountain pens also popped up all over the place. As did matching ink splotches on shirt pockets.

One day, eighth-grader J.D. came to school wearing a Christmas present, a turtleneck sweater, obviously a couple sizes too small. Nobody returned Christmas gifts in those days.

Anyhow, that afternoon, with four walls of stuffiness closing in, J.D. began the long, twisting struggle of pulling the sweater up and over his head. Poor kid, he might've done himself in if two Boy Scouts hadn't bolted to his aid. Unforgettable drama.

Ah, and how can I forget winsome E.K., who, upon arriving at school, switched her new charm bracelet to her ankle? Quite a daring, seductive exhibition in its day.

She met E.E. in a secluded corner of a hall while the remainder of the student body romped innocently in the schoolyard during recess. There, she folded up her skirt slightly, and extended her leg to give him a close-up of her new anklet. Then they kissed. *Honest!*

I didn't eyewitness the infamous buss, but somehow our principal, the omnipresent Mother Superior, beheld the whole sordid affair. Enraged, she penned a formal letter and handed it to E.K. in the middle of a class, with instructions that the girl have her parents sign it and bring it back in the morning.

According to several utterly reliable sources, the nun's letter concluded: "Then, right there in the hall, your daughter had the audacity to kiss this boy after brazenly raising her skirt and showing him her bangle."

Took me a month to figure out what a bangle was.

Gertrude Was a Stitch

$\mathcal{L}$ast time I wrote about Gertrude, she got sore at me. The occasion? Her ninetieth birthday.

"Now that everybody knows how *old* I am," said she, peevishly, "they'll be wanting to *do* things for me."

Well, if *anyone* was going to be doing something for somebody, Gertrude wanted to be the doer. That's the way she was.

And, by the way, there wasn't anything the diminutive widow couldn't do with needle and thread. Or trowel and pruning shears, while we're at it.

If she'd kept records of all the clothes she made and gave away, and all the neighborhood alteration jobs performed, she would've had a drawer bulging with due bills.

She was a seamstress by love.

She lived just down the road, and when her husband died three decades ago, my wife practically adopted her as a mother. She'd call Gertrude, ask if she wanted to accompany her on an errand, and the lady'd be ready to go at the drop of a stitch.

"I'll be outside in ten minutes," she'd say.

Gertrude was funny, read voraciously, but she lived frugally in her cottage—by choice.

Not until a few years ago did she indulge and have central air conditioning installed. Even then she switched it on infrequently.

On a stifling, mid-summer's afternoon, she coyly informed a surprise, drop-in visitor, "Oh, it seems to be getting a little warm. Think I should turn on the air?"

And then one day, almost overnight, Gertrude was ninety-nine years old, still living alone—by obdurate personal choice—and preparing her own nutritious meals, doing the cleaning, laundry, entertaining members of her garden club.

The only difference now, she was deaf and legally blind, and the light was fading from her heart. Her fingertips were worn, but her mind was sharp as a needle.

And then one recent night, she had a great fall on her front porch and broke her hip.

Her two daughters, living in faraway places, were notified. Meantime, her closest neighbors, a physician and his wife, and a pair of academic doctors, keeping tight, loving surveillance on her as always, rallied round.

At that point I think we began doubting she'd live to salute the year 2000 or celebrate her 100th birthday.

Even when Gertrude could no longer stroll our road, it was crucial for us to know she was in that house—a symbol of intelligent independence and good old-fashioned American pluck.

In her last lucid moments in the hospital, she clearly conceded that her days as an independent woman were up.

Born in rambunctious Chicago, May 1900, she died in a quiet fifth-floor room in Orlando Regional Medical Center as the days of October dwindled down in the year of Our Lord 1999.

Kissing her goodbye in the hospital the last time, my wife said she'd see her the next day.

Gertrude said she wouldn't be there.

So where would she be?

"Home. I'll be home."

Her family has asked my wife to deliver Gertrude's eulogy.

All the flags on our road are flying half-mast.

Leona Herself

*D*ishes came and went pleasantly. The women ate and chatted and laughed together, and laughed even heartier when the waiter suggested desserts. The laughter ceased after the waiter added up the damages and presented just one check to the table.

Now, tabulating individual checks for a group of, say, half a dozen or more, can be a nuisance, I suppose. People in the business, however, should be inured to this sort of request, and, indeed, on this occasion, this particular server showed no discernible sign of resistance when so instructed at the outset.

A dear friend of mine, an author, was acting spokesperson for these diners, and has been around long enough to know when she's been fast-shuffled. Grabbing the retreating waiter's coattail, so to speak, she called, "Whoa there, laddie." Patiently she reiterated her case for separate checks, but the fellow, smoothing the wrinkles of his displaced dignity, played the part of a dumb waiter, literally.

His response was sheer gobbledygook. In essence: "Sorry, madam, that's the way it is," and off he vanished behind the kitchen's swinging doors. No, that's not the way it was at all. Dramatically my friend swung after him into the kitchen and dealt him a free, colorful piece of her mind in front of his spellbound coworkers.

All this took place in the dining room of a downtown Orlando hotel more than two decades ago. I bring up the scene today because warm visions of it, and other impromptu skits and food served there over the years, danced in my head when I learned that the place is preparing to shut down. Business has fallen off. For one woeful reason or another. Oh, how I abhor that, another of our mainstay lodgings biting the sand.

Anyhow, to complete the tale, the author, upon arriving home, strode straight to her computer to compose a stiff letter regarding the waiter. Her novel-in-the-works could wait. She addressed her document to the then hotel owner in New York: Leona Helmsley.

Leona, herself, in no time at all, got back to the Orlando woman via telephone. "Oh, my *dear!*" she gushed sympathetically into her ear in a husky voice of pure velour.

Although details of the ensuing telephone discourse, once divulged to me, have been deleted by time, Leona's colossal opening words—those three breathy little words, burnished with grandiloquence and an overload of compassion—remain ingrained in my brain. Was this the same Leona Helmsley, oft' depicted by the media as a ruthless businesswoman, the one labeled "Queen of Mean," now reaching across one thousand miles to pat the hand of a lone dining room guest? Yes, I know she spent twenty-one months up the river for tax evasion, but I stand ready to forgive and forget that.

And offer thanks for her grand little gesture of long ago. If she were here I'd take her hands, look in her eyes and say, with all the grandiloquence and compassion I could muster, "Oh, my *dear!*"

Hear the Blind Man's Solo

*F*requently on summer evenings as we ate supper in the kitchen, we heard the approaching sound of the blind man's oboe solo.

Or, on some of Midwest's sultrier twilights, we might be supping on the screened porch as the musician advanced. Always he traversed the sidewalk across the street, left to right, roughly fifty yards from our porch. We never learned his name, or his point of origin, although in the span of a few years, he'd become a familiar character.

Perhaps a relative or friend chauffeured him to a place nearby by, then routinely picked him up following his strolling, money-raising recital. Maybe he'd hazarded out on his own, disembarking from a streetcar on the boulevard a block away, and eventually circling through the neighborhood back to the tracks.

Now, all at once, seventy years have passed. It's a Monday evening. And after toting recyclable items and a bag of garbage to the side of the road, I stand outside our cottage for a gentle minute. Here, before stepping back inside to watch a movie with my wife, I draw the softening colors of the Southern sky and all the trustworthy sounds of summer's gloaming into my arms.

And for a moment, for one mystical moment, with eyes closed, I believe I can also hear it again, the sound of the blind man's oboe serenade.

Lawdy, how exalted the fellow would've been to know that the echo of his horn would carry a thousand miles and well over half a century.

On the other hand, alas, it pains me that I can't also relate that the man was a gifted musician, or simply that he could carry a tune. You've heard of haunting melodies. This fellow sounded as if he were *hunting* for melodies. Never would he measure up for the job of strolling musician in an elegant restaurant or a neighborhood beer garden. His signature sound was loud, artless, tinny.

That's the taxing part of this plot. Yet, in a way, it's irrelevant.

No one questioned his sincerity. He showed up regularly in dark glasses. Fastened to his belt were a tin cup and a white cane. And he played his heart out as though he were a child prodigy.

If one of my two brothers or I darted across to drop a few pennies or a nickel in his cup, he'd mutter a thank-you, then be on his way, cheeks puffing, a musician on a mission.

So I'm ready to rejoin my wife in our cottage now, but I linger, listening to squirrels bedding down, raccoons rustling for a night on the town, the muted hum of the toll road, the all-is-well bark of a dog, the day preparing to turn the page.

And closer, unforgettably clear and important in the sundown of memory, is the forlorn howl of the oboe, played by a man who'd never witnessed the beauty of dusk, a musician who'd never heard applause.

And then one summer he was gone.

Here's to Everybody

Stepping out at an invigorating pace along a shady street this morning, my wife and I spied a woman emerging from her home. As we called our regards to her, I doffed my broad-brimmed straw hat.

"Oh," said she, a beaming woman in the seventy to eighty bracket, "you don't see much of *that* anymore. A gentleman from the old school."

Although no one ever trained me in this, the art of tipping a hat to a woman as a courtly gesture, I watched my dad do it enough to learn the routine. Even when he and Mom were out promenading and encountered a man by himself coming their way on the sidewalk, Dad's fingers instinctively reached to his headdress. Ditto when he went by a church—whether on foot or if careening past in a packed street car.

Personally, I've had little use over the years for headgear. Except, naturally, in the 1940s army.

Well, sure, when playing sandlot baseball too. No gamy, self-respecting kid would ever think of stepping up to the plate bareheaded. How could you possibly be serious about getting a base hit if you didn't have a bill to pull down and practically cover your peepers?

Last year my wife bought me this straw hat with the oversized brim. We're blessed with a shady neighborhood in which to exert ourselves, but those barbarous islands of subtropical sun are the devil to dodge. So there I stood in the middle of the street—no sidewalks here and the traffic is scant—and I swept off my hat and felt a tree-sweetened breeze through my damp hair.

In that moment, in that suddenly exalted instant, lifting

my lid also served as a wild and silent wave to my dad, and to all the women he ever tipped his hat to, including my mom. And to all the mannerly men—in the short while they walked among us—who made life a little lighter for others. Who made us smile. It was a bubble of a moment only, and I felt surrounded by the world of decency.

Alas, as everybody knows, you can't stand in the middle of the road forever. And so, as my wife and I skipped along, I pondered the woman's words. "A gentleman from the old school." I smiled. I've heard that phrase with some recurrence of late. The *old* school. Has me wondering. Have I always been old? Seriously, folks, I'm proud to be an alum of that school, but, please, don't think me a prisoner of the "good old days," either. I still have my heart set, thank you, on a little more higher learning.

OK, here's what I'd like to do right now. Clear off my desk. Don my straw hat. Step outside. And from the middle of the gravel driveway, doff the hat to you and to everyone else in the world at large who's sharing a little light music with me today. That's my intention, and that's the truth.

Soon as it stops raining.

Sheets in the Wind

No telling how many hundreds of times I've heard sudden, rolling thunder outside my home.

So can someone please tell me why, on a rumbling day most recent, I quizzed myself thusly, "If it's about to rain, shouldn't I be taking some sort of emergency measure, like bringing in the laundry off the line in the backyard?" Or words to that effect. It happened so rapidly, see, I can't precisely recall each syllable.

In any event, it's the *thought* that counts, and that was the thought—forever whatever quirky reason—that went off in my head.

It's true, despite the reality that there were no clothes hanging in the yard at the time; nor, indeed, has there even been a clothes*line* in any yard where I've dwelt since the curtain rang down on World War II.

Well, obviously, those unanticipated Monday thunderstorms of long-ago summers—the plague for my mom and for all the housewives from one end of our block to the other—left an indelible etching on my youthful soul. Burps of thunder or isolated trinkets of rain touching down on rooftops sent the good women scurrying to the outdoors with their wicker laundry baskets, eyes on the dubious sky, skirts flying. Some housewives, after hanging out wash on overcast days, risked a run over to the corner grocery store. Others, swayed by sunny skies, swung aboard a bus or streetcar for a couple hours of shopping downtown.

If a full rain did fall while they were off the premises, this was the signal for neighbors to demonstrate their— well, neighborliness.

Ah, quite the sight to behold, the women, and any youngsters they could corral, running next door or across the brick street to unpin someone's laundry and tote it to the nearest shelter—and all of us tickled silly to pitch in.

You always went for the bed sheets first, the big items. It's something the savvy kid picks up.

Something else one gleans over the years is that apparently there are two well-defined camps of thought on the manner of drying sheets. This is very important.

Laundresses of one faction preach that nothing's more invigorating or sleep-inducing—after a hot bath—than to turn in at night on linens that have been warmed by the sun and blown by the wind that very day.

Hard-shelled opponents who pooh-pooh the procedure insist that sheets and pillowcases tumbling out of an automatic dryer are softer, silkier, sleepier.

I can close my eyes on either picture for mere seconds, and find myself drowsing.

Now, before I rock-a-bye off to Slumbersville, I feel compelled to salute the many *men* today who also do the family laundry. On my street in my kiddy days, the wives and moms jealously handled that task.

The men, meanwhile, were at work. Either that, or they were out *looking* for work—the sad dads who didn't sleep so well at night, no matter how the sheets were dried.

A Stranger Pulls Up

Oh, what a beautiful Sunday morning,
and there I sat on the venerable wooden steps of my grandma's front porch.

Life was pretty nifty back in my childish days, although I probably didn't put it into so many words then.

At the moment I was eyeing a parade of slicked-up folks on the sidewalk and mounting the broad steps of a church over on the corner across the street. I'd already been to church that morning, a church of a different denomination.

Parked automobiles and an occasional pickup occupied both sides of the narrow brick pavement. Gradually the churchgoers thinned out. Suddenly a car stopped directly below me, and the driver, an old guy about forty, beckoned me to his vehicle. I approached no closer than the sidewalk.

"Hey, kid," an unlit cigarette bobbing on his lips, "got a match?"

When I shook my head negatively, he advised me to go in the house and fetch him a couple. "Step it up."

Step it up? Listen, I couldn't beat it out of there fast enough and around the house.

Did I go inside Grandma's and fetch a handful of her kitchen matches? If that's what you think I did, you got another thing coming.

See, I *knew* the rogue was up to something funny. The minute I stuck my hand in the car window he'd absolutely clutch my wrist, haul me inside, and drive me off for some dastardly purpose.

No, I didn't tip off Grandma, either. No need her getting all roiled up. My own heart was going like sixty.

So I hid behind the house, every so often peeking out front. At last, incredulously, just before he drove away, I watched the suspicious character produce a match and light his cigarette.

I *knew* I'd been right. He'd been up to no good.

Naturally he'd spoiled my Sunday morning. No longer could I horse around out front, just sit out there looking about, fearing he might be circling the block.

My age at the time? Can't say, but surely I'd been coached not to have any truck with strangers. Therefore, this might've been my first real *live* brush with someone who was not enamored of my boyish good looks and outlook. Bit of a shock? Indeed. All in all, admittedly, if nothing else, I'd say it was a sound experience to start me getting saddled up for life.

Here in my study today, I wonder if there's a boy or girl out there, same age as I on that old Sunday morn, worried, puzzled by the fear and pandemonium loose in the world.

Well, the kid must understand. Funny stuff and rumors of funny stuff are all part of the deal. You can't hide behind Grandma's house forever, but it's going to be all right. It really is.

Meantime, I pray there's a warm, aromatic kitchen in this youngster's life, somewhere to duck into, to be coddled by the spectacle of a grandma sliding a crumb coffee cake from the oven.

The Voice Next Door

Let's say we're in attendance at a banquet. The toastmaster, before calling up the principal speaker, is reeling off the names of some of the other assembled notables. Pausing dramatically now, he looks up from his list, and intones, "We would also like to honor a special gentleman who is here with us on this most auspicious night, Mr. So-And-So, who turned *one hundred* today!"

The audience gasps, smiles, laughs and gives him a standing ovation—yes, even those banqueteers who have no clue as to who this So-And-So is.

Plainly, folks, there's something about the age of one hundred that merits our awes and applause. No other age comes anywhere near to rousing that sort of spontaneous personal emotion in people—unless, of course, it's ninety-nine.

Or, in certain circumstances, eleven.

Certain circumstances?

Well, yes, such as a certain newspaper columnist remarking in the public prints that the spirited girl in residence next door is eleven, when she is actually twelve, just one small step away from coveted teenhood.

Chances are I wouldn't gave gotten wind of my inexcusable faux pas if the man of the house next door hadn't hopped over last night to borrow an egg. While here, he alluded to one of my recent columns, the one in which I assumed he and his wife had forgiven my spouse and me for not yet reading the *Harry Potter* book they gave us for Christmas.

"We forgive you," said the affable neighbor, "but I don't

know if my daughter is ready to forgive you for saying she's only eleven. Maybe some day she will, but not just yet."

I should've known better. Oh, absolutely. If I'd really revved up my mind, I would've recalled that it was an early evening late in the summer of '89 when the couple next to our cottage arrived home from the hospital. This was back when I was only a rookie in the retirement game, and happened to be watering a row of bushes in the front yard as their car—it was a *family* car now—came chugging into their driveway.

Ah, what a picture, the mother in the back seat, the tiny bundle of the two-day-old daughter cribbed preciously in her arms. Behold, there was suddenly new blood in the old neighborhood.

As memory reveals, I expressed in print the desire that I'd still be around to see the girl sashay down our road one day all dolled up, stepping out in her first party dress.

Well, I did stand witness to that gorgeous scene, and to several other sightings and blessings, her first day off to school and so on.

And frequently I heard her winning little voice pipe up from behind trees and foliage, or from the open window of a vehicle, "Hi, Ed!"

I haven't heard that call recently, well over a year, as the blossoming young lady next door prances to catch up with the teenagers. And I miss it.

Taking The Pledge

Whole days go by when I fail to step out on our sundeck.

It's true. Without standing there. Without inhaling the celestial pigmentation of the sky and the configurations of the clouds. That's right, without once showing up for a spiritual refill, not even for a fly-by moment to salute my priceless collection of Elysian artwork reflected in the private lake below.

Think of it. Whole days without the blessings.

I'm abstaining from turning in any New Year's resolutions this time around, but if I were of a mind to do so, certainly a pledge to pass more of my minutes out on the deck would be somewhere near the top of the list.

I simply must find the time—or generate it—to step on out there and breathe, that's all.

You know, when people sign up for Social Security paychecks, you'd think they'd have a barrel of spare moments to choose from for these bracing moments. Somehow it doesn't quite unfold in this fashion.

My kid brother, who's only seventy-six, and I, were standing around in my driveway chewing the fat about this subject one morning last week. In truth, we were sharing a quiet guffaw about our crammed timetables, and marveling about how in the dickens we ever fulfilled so many extracurricular obligations back in our ancient times of time-clock punching.

"In fact, with so many obligations these days," he said, "I often feel a little punch drunk."

Granted, my brother has been known to yield to the

facetious hyperbole, but he does make a sober point.

By and large, we have only ourselves to slap the blame on. He made his way in life mostly as a singer and showman, and is still willingly and harmoniously involved in the nearly fulltime practice of his professional art.

And I'm still writing stories on deadline. After half a century, it's a hard habit to bust.

No, I doubt I'll be fashioning a docket of resolutions for the forthcoming year. Still, if I do happen to feel the urge to draw one up for old times' sake, definitely the pledge to get together more frequently with my little brother will also be high on the list. It's a mere half-hour's drive over to his place, and, after all, he's not going to be around forever.

After these multitudinous years it's splendid to discover we still relish one another's company. When we stand around in the driveway we don't lift the hoods of our vehicles and kick tires. We talk and we laugh about the roads we've traveled, and about those we hope yet to wander.

I don't mind telling you that this boy and I slept in the same bed up in the attic of our old house, up in featherbed heaven, and when the blitz of winter hit, we huddled together like a pair of newborn puppies.

And it was good.

But for his wife's sake, I hope his feet have warmed up.

Cousins Forever

My old gang is breaking up.

There were five of us originally, including my two brothers and our two cousins. Sure, we collected other chums in time, but this was a particularly close branch of the family tree, pals by birth, pals by choice. Before World War II sent us scrambling to converse fields, we lived in the same neighborhood, and felt at home in any of our three houses.

And now, just four of us. Cousin Jack died last week. He was almost 80, but to me he was, and still is, Jackie.

We hadn't spoken eyeball-to-eyeball in years, but his passing was a stunning left hook to the midriff. We'd been boys together, see, he being only a few months older than I, and as an only child he virtually lived at our place. Now, he's no longer around. A lifetime swept by in a blink. If those two thoughts don't make a person ponder one's mortality in a hurry, what will?

Most rapaciously I remember the merry Christmas Eves at Grandma's gift-wrapped house. Jackie was a tinseled part of all that—until it was put away for the duration. The cousins joined the war, one by one. But we came home again, thank God. There were still more critical assignments to carry out.

One day, Jackie showed up at our house with a beautiful young woman in hand. "Meet Doris," he said. Obviously he was hooked for life. My cousin, an only child, wedded Doris and became the father of six children; and there are 16 *grand* chips off the old block, at last count.

But before settling into that, he joined me for a vacation in Los Angeles where I was striving to attain movie stardom. We caught a train to San Diego to visit my older brother, still in the navy, and he chaperoned us to Tijuana, showed us the sights, even shelled out for hotel accommodations. The only catch, the three of us spent the night in the same bed built for two. Jackie slept like a log—with his right arm under my pillow all night.

Alas, there's one boyhood scene I wish I could forget. We were about ten, eleven, playing football in our backyard. For some niggling reason, Jackie and I shifted into a wrestling match, and I made him say uncle. Then it was time for us brothers to go in, wash up for supper.

Jackie turned for the gate. Nothing passed between us, not a handshake, smile, or a so long. He was gone.

I see him, head bowed, sprigs of autumn grass clinging to his sweater, slouching down the alley in the dusk, no brothers to talk it over with on the long walk home.

Oh, if I could play that scene over, I'd dart to the gate, and in my high clear voice cry out to the forlorn, fading figure: "Jackie! Come back! Jackie? Come back, Jackie!"

Where'd All the Sailors Go?

*P*eople, people everywhere, and not a sailor in sight.

This was the missing ingredient on a recent, rare evening of retail adventure, as I strode the concourse at our town's Fashion Square. In years past, this is where one could get a close-up look at the boys and girls—make that young men and women—who once graced our fair village in uniforms of the US Navy.

Not much of a hike from the front gate of Orlando Naval Training Center, so here's where many recruits converged when awarded the sporadic hour of freedom from the exactitudes of boot camp.

Bright and polite. That's what I remember foremost about them, either by contact or simply from the sidelines.

An old-fashioned sort, I rather like hearing "Yes, sir" from out of the mouths of young persons. Or, come to that, even "No, sir."

They arrived at the base from the four corners of this country, and beyond, to learn, to tune up, and obviously had something worthwhile themselves to share, to leave behind.

I can't say if they fled to the mall to shop, or for nostalgic browsing. If a portion ganged up merely to leer at constituents of the opposite sex, who could blame them? Our town is renowned for its attractive members of both strains.

Unquestionably they had it better than we soldiers did back in ole Virginny in '43. When briefly emancipated from basic training, we'd strip off our fatigues, dress up in khakis, and grab a bus for the nearby small town.

There, we'd ankle up and down the civilian sidewalks that were jam-packed with more soldiers, and after a couple hours of that revelry, loosen our ties for the bus ride back to camp.

I can't recall when last I paid an evening visit to this Orlando mall, and I'd forgotten that the naval facility has already been closed for eight years.

Naturally I never walked the concourse just to notice the boys and girls in their immaculate whites, but there they were to behold, and I smiled at them, the true faces of our land, eager, sound, idealistic.

I felt the same uplifting swagger of spirit and pride each time I drove by their training center. Things were going on inside those fences to the rhythm of unseen pulses, ensuring that ours would remain the most proficient and powerful navy the world has ever known.

Every Friday morning for almost thirty years the gates swung open to residents and to families of the grads, to come fill the bleachers and watch the recruits pass in review.

Who didn't shiver, even on the hottest of days, when the Navy Band of Orlando, Bluejacket Chorus, the fifty-state flag team, and two precision drill teams hit the field to give the polished young people a so-long salute?

This was America on parade. More than 650,000 of them walked this way.

The other night I strode the mall, and looked—and not a sailor in sight.

Where'd they all go? I miss them.

She Keeled Over Alone

And now, finally, it's gone. The tree.

It keeled over on a recent morning, with no one standing witness.

Evidently my wife and I were the only persons within earshot as the trunk thumped to the rain-pulped turf. The sound drew us outside from our respective rooms where we work and muse; and there, across the road on the edge of the small, wooded estate, stood the empty space where the mighty paper tree once proudly sprouted. Or the *melaleuca,* if you fancy the more scholarly designation of this strain.

Oh, Lord, how the little people did cherish that tree in its heyday.

It was never a climbing tree, and sported no configuration for a tree house; ah, but the light-hued bark could be peeled away like sheets of an oversized tablet.

From all I ever heard, the boys and girls viewed it as having been planted exclusively for them—an unending supply of slates on which to engrave initials and hearts and to scrawl notices of the imperative "I love Betty Ann" variety.

Because there are no sidewalks on our dead-end road, the tree stood within convenient reach of passersby. Additionally, the grip of close-by oaks and bamboo formulated a sort of hideaway for the juvenile set.

Reassuringly, there was never a report of some underhanded kid using a carving instrument, bold marker or felt-point pen to efface the majestic trunk with a repugnant word or sketch.

But, alas, the tree hadn't yielded any fresh bark for well over a decade, and neighbors began to wonder if it was the fault of the work corps that showed up one day to saw off the high-reaching arms interfering with electrical wires.

Perhaps it was just too old to produce? Possibly it was a simple matter of neighborhood demographics, but whatever the reason, the boys and girls had stopped coming to visit.

If you ask me, the tree missed the kids. What'd become of all the chatter and the laughter and that haphazard pile of parked bicycles?

The melaleuca began to look neglected. Like an old, confused woman defrocked of her blossom, that's what she was, and trying to figure out why the world was sashaying by without as much as a nod.

Finally, after living on begged and borrowed time, and legend, the decayed twenty-foot trunk spent all its hope, and toppled over, neatly, without fuss. It lay on the easement, as if placed there by a surveyor, out of harm's way, on a line directly parallel with the road.

As an erudite neighbor would later observe, "She died like a lady."

Within the hour another corps of workmen was on the scene, this time to hoist the remains into the bed of a truck. The men swept up, then the truck moved on down the road, leaving nothing behind, not even a shadow, nothing except all the silent echoes of messages left on deposit with the paper tree.

Only two people waved goodbye.

Dad's Cup Runneth Dry

*B*efore *hiking off to high school in the* morning, I'd carry a cup of hot coffee downstairs to my dad who was minding the store.

One blustery morning, my selfish mind overloaded with juvenile matters, I forgot to deliver his treat. Not until about a mile from our flat and store did I remember. Numbed by my thoughtlessness and the wind, I stood there, frozen in place. So *that's* why he'd looked at me a little oddly, sadly, as I'd left the confectionery and waved so long.

It's the kind of day you recall down the road, and wish you could go back to it, redo it.

Being tardy for school was no calamity, but had I retraced my steps that icy day, Dad would've been truly unnerved. He was not a shopkeeper by trade, my dad. He'd worked in accounting during most of the Depression, luckily, for Shell Petroleum. And then one gloomy day got his walking papers.

That same scenario of social insecurity is playing today, firms cutting back. Suddenly breadwinners who thought they were fixed for life are out pounding pavements.

Hard times. That says it all.

One thing, Dad did walk away with some severance cash, but it vanished in a flash.

A friend, who reminded him that he was no longer a spring rooster, talked him into buying a certain "gold mine" confectionery. "Be your own boss."

Essentially it was a mom-and-pop store—a term unfamiliar to my dad, fortunately. If there was one thing in this world he abhorred, it was being called *Pop*.

So, at last he was his own boss, although it meant he

was handcuffed to that building seven days and nights per week. Even when we locked up early Sunday afternoon for dinner, people thumped on the door, or stood on the sidewalk and called up to us that they needed salt, a bottle of milk, a roll of bathroom tissue.

Business wasn't bad. Actually, it was too brisk when you measured the hours and labor against the lean line of profit.

I remember an old woman who came in once a week for a loaf of bread, and always demanded a bag. One day, Dad stuck it in an old paper-handled tote that'd last carried six bottles of beer. She sniffed, sashayed out with the bag advertising Budweiser, and never came back.

Well, in time, as the hours and work stacked up, and with nothing saved, Dad began losing his grand sense of humor. There. That's the tragedy. The statistic that doesn't show up in the business news.

How often had he longed to be back doing what he did best?

In a few years my folks practically gave the store away, and, thank God, with no debts outstanding.

I pray that today's job-seekers fare better than did my dad. He ultimately regained his droll ways, but never again found a job worthy of his singular tools and talents.

He'd gone for the gold, and come away empty-handed.

And one cup of coffee short.

Alley Hoops

$\mathcal{F}$*ather and daughter are engrossed in a* project together.

It's a warming sight indeed on this chilly, ashen, Sunday afternoon in early January.

Their dual aim is to erect her Christmas gift, a basketball backboard, goal and base, in their driveway—optimistically before another Christmas rolls round.

It's no snap job. The implements come with pages of instructions, as I alertly observed while peeking at the neighbors through the spreading, leafy viburnum that separates our properties.

Really I should offer to assist the conversant chap, but after we've resided side-by-side for more than a decade, he's well aware that I have no hopes of ever being enshrined as a legendary handyman.

Besides, my vigor ain't what it used to be. I can picture myself going over there to lend a hand, then excusing myself in short order on the grounds that it's time for my nap.

Right, and after all, who wants to be shown up by a pretty twelve-year-old *girl?*

The proceedings next door do flash merry images in my head, reminders of an earlier year, much earlier, when our neighborhood gang gathered in the narrow alley behind my grandma's house for some grand, Midwest basketball action.

Most of us fellows would be putting on the uniforms of war any day, so maybe that's why we played with such abandon and full-throated delight.

Oh, boy, wouldn't we have cherished a genuine backboard and a goal with a net to shoot at, instead of a bottomless, honest-to-goodness peach basket nailed to Grandma's lean-to shed? That's where we staged our sharp-shooting contests of horse, one-on-one, and half-court matches, playing our hearts out, romping for the utter love of the game, and each other, the setting, the time.

Those were the days when the bulk of basketball's points were rung up on swift lay-ups, two-handed set shots, and those funny underhanded free throws.

Nowhere I know of are there any record books on those skirmishes of old in the alley, but it matters not a whit. In the long run all that counts is the gorgeous, teeming camaraderie.

Now, just a minute ago, I arose from my workbench chair, and stepped outside the house. It's twilight, and evidently my neighbors have put away their tools. The basketball platform and pole are up. The backboard and basket await another day. Rich memories take time.

Back in my study, my eyes closed, I take one more look down the alley.

Game's over. It's cold now and the players tug their jackets and sweaters back on and stand around talking about everything important and nothing at all. This is the best part.

Finally we drift apart. Suppers are waiting.

The kid who owns the basketball trods up the alley alone, slowly bouncing the ball as he goes, thump, thump, thump, the sound fading into the gloaming. He turns in at a gate.

He's gone.

Crossed Her Fingers and Hoped

My mom was a big believer in the crossing of fingers as a means to an end.

Superstitious, you say?

Sure, possibly, but in her lifetime she would never have employed that word—not regarding herself. She was also an unwavering believer in the potency of prayer, and in which she found solace, right up to the end—thirty-seven years ago this week. The difference, I think, is that she relied on petitions and devices of less spiritual disposition when the problem at hand fell far below the life-or-death classification. In short, any request she didn't want to bother God with.

Even so, often were the times I'd see her blessing herself in the kitchen, say immediately prior to sliding a loaf of bread or a three-layer cake into the oven.

Of course, the voracious way her three sons dug in at the supper table, a guest might've *sensed* a prevailing life-or-death quality in that room.

Anyhow, my wife and I were discussing superstitions, after reading in our newspaper about a young fella named A.J. Pierzynski who played baseball while attending an Orlando high school. And who is now paid handsomely by the Minnesota Twins for playing the same game. See what a high school education can do for a person?

The newspaper story focused on the young man's parents, sitting tensely in their favorite positions by the TV, watching him perform a leading role in the American League Championship Series. Superstition, the word, was not mentioned in the piece. Implications, however, were rife.

"I know what anguish the boy's parents were going through," I sagely remarked to my wife, who claims to be superstition free.

My older brother was also a baseballer, you see, a pitcher of big-time promise in high school. Mom couldn't just sit in the bleachers. Oh, no. She'd appear to be wringing her hanky, but was really engaged in sophisticated maneuvers of crossing her fingers. If my brother found himself in a jam on the hill, she'd cross her index and middle finger and sit on the hand.

My dad plainly couldn't sit still. He'd roam behind the bleachers or stroll the left-field foul line, face turned up to the sun, straw hat in hand. Every so often he'd look back to see how his son was faring.

By the way, saying my wife is free of superstitions isn't the whole truth. Out of deference to me she never reveals her dreams *before* breakfast—a little omen I picked up from Mom.

Actually, I'm not superstitious. OK, I make sure to put on my left sock first, and walk around the Confederate jasmine bush on the lawn before getting in my car. But those hardly count.

Well, Mom had a painful time of it toward the end, but her face was tranquil last time I saw her as she lay in her final resting place, in prayerful pose, a rosary entwined in her hands. And all ten of her fingers were crossed.

House with Bath

Amid all the perturbing news in the nation's periodicals, a story quietly materializes regarding the evolution of the American home.

This subject has fascinated me going quite a way back—well, back to the time when I was a bawling babe in my dad's rocking arms, and he walked the floor with me in the middle of many a night.

Today I also ponder: What despairing thoughts might've stomped through Dad's head in those exhausting wee hours if he'd known that he and Mom were destined to bring still another son, their third, into diaper world?

Unanswerable questions aside, the newspaper story points out that we need only to look in the bathroom to understand how much the typical American home has changed in sixty-odd years. Approximately half of U.S. homes when I was a boy, according to the Census Bureau, had a "complete system" bathroom—hot water, flush toilet, and bathtub. Our family slipped into the lower half.

Wait, it could've been worse. Luckily, we were one social step above having to use an outhouse.

Although we called the room off the kitchen our bathroom, no bathtub was included. There was a flush toilet, and that was it. Oh, plus the square, high-set window looking out upon the branches of a cherry tree. Believe me, it was a millionaire's view.

One thing we never did was wash our hands before leaving the bathroom. True, that's a deplorable habit, but you see, there was no washbasin in there. Emerging users were expected to handle that soapy matter at the kitchen sink. In a way, that was better, allowing Mom to see that we followed proper hygienic procedures.

Hot and cold running water was a major selling point in real estate in the '20s and '30s. Our house had both. Hot water in summer, cold in winter.

Bathwater was heated either on the coal-burning stove or the gas range. Actually, you didn't need much for splashing about in a galvanized washtub.

I remember my mom in the kitchen on those late Saturday afternoons, lowering the shades on the side window and the back door to imbue each bather with a sense of privacy. The week was winding down then, and we were scrubbing up for supper, early bed, and church in the morning. Funny, how a simple routine can transform into an aching excitement in the recollection.

My friends down at the Census Bureau can tell about the nation's bathrooms, how many telephones and bedrooms we have now on the average and all that, but they're missing the better half in the story of the evolution of the home—us.

Regardless, here's a hopeful prayer that I wasn't a ghastly pain in the ears to my dad as he cradled and walked me back and forth in one of America's statistical bedrooms.

For the record, I never felt more secure than whenever that man wrapped me in his warm, strong arms. No matter my age.

Grandma's Spooky Dungeon

Once upon a time I thought it was Grandma's mission in life to keep her grandkids supplied with slices of sweet surprises.

On days when there was nothing in her oven except our snow-wet mittens drying out, even then we could count on being treated to something off the shelf in her pantry.

But there was a catch.

Occasionally I'd be dispatched to the cellar to fetch a jar of homemade preserves.

No, I was not a child who expected to be waited on hand and foot, as the saying goes. I didn't expect anything of the sort until fifty or so years later—after I retired.

Truthfully, I rather relished racking up points by performing Herculean chores for my widowed maternal Grandma—like laying in kindling for her kitchen and bedroom stoves, emptying ashes, and carrying in a bucket of coal in each hand from the shed.

But listen. I would rather have been upended in a roller-skate hockey game out on our brick street than be invited to take a solo trip down into that spooky, unlighted, dirt cellar.

You reached the dungeon by a door in Grandma's bedroom. At least that's where you stood *thinking* about going down, where you stood remembering Bela Lugosi and Boris Karloff movies, where you could smell the timeless arms of cold, dank earth opening for you.

For all I knew, evil lurked in the shadows below. Grandma offered a candle, but of what use would that be to a boy who'd be making the trip down and back with his eyes closed?

If a feller had to learn to take the bitter with the sweet in life, Grandma's was sure the place to be.

Well, I guess we all—especially those with multiple years draped around us—have our childhood stories of horror to tell. Just this week when the domestic subject of basements came up, my wife recalled how she had recoiled when directed by her aunt to go downstairs to retrieve some item. And this in a *finished* basement and a light to show the way. She had it easy. Still, she had to be virtually pushed into it.

Her aunt would say, "What can happen to you? I'll be standing right up here."

Sure, but how would that help, her aunt a flight of stairs away, if the girl came face to face with a burglar who'd slipped in through the coal chute?

Like most dwellers in subtropical Florida, my wife and I have no basement. Believe me, she wouldn't have it any other way.

Back in the 1930s up north, some of my wealthier relatives made fruitful use of their full basements, cooking and eating their main meals of summertime down in the cooler environs.

And yet, after cleaning up, and lights out, and the family back upstairs, who knew what stirred below ground level, skulked under the staircase, behind the furnace?

What happened to all those bugbears of our youth that never jumped out to get us? Are they still lurking, still waiting?

Called

Read All About It

I've labored in the newspaper business since I was eleven years old. By my current reckoning, it means I started sixty-seven years ago. No matter how you look at it, even if my calculations are off a notch or two, that's quite a run.

Naturally I didn't land any choice writing assignments right off the bat. Actually, I got my feet wet—literally—in the circulation department. All right, so that's also a bit of a stretch. Truth is, I began as an assistant to my older brother on his Sunday newspaper delivery route.

Even so, ever since that first day—and a frigid December morn it was—the Sunday edition of newspapers has been one of my favorite things.

Oh lawdy, how my boyish eyes nearly popped their sockets when we reached the delivery substation on my inaugural outing, and I beheld an alp of newspapers. Wrapped in their colorful comic sections, they were stacked clear to the ceiling of that old wooden shack.

Wending our empty, two-wheeled wagon from home had been an onerous enough chore along the nine blocks of those lamp-lit, ice-pocked St. Louis streets. Loaded down with fifty papers, the going was, well, excuse the language, treacherous as blazes.

Finally, somewhere down the line of that damp, pre-dawn morn, my brother slyly let me check the list of customer addresses myself and allowed me to make my first deposit.

Mounting the sparkling porch steps, carrying the newspaper as carefully as a butler walking in with a turkey on a silver platter, I heard a dog snarl, then bark. Dogs and I did not make fast friends in those yonder days, but fear not, I wasn't planning to lollygag around that station, just stuff the paper behind the storm door and scoop up the dime from the bowl and be long gone.

The barking, from inside the house, increased in volume and viciousness as the dog came raging down a long hallway and took a flying leap at me. Fortunately there was a door between us. If the pooch broke any glass, I can't honestly say. I was already down the steps, doing a bit of yelping myself, and up to the next house where my brother stood innocently waiting.

Oh, sure, waiting and trying to hold back his laughter.

Yup, I'd been initiated. Not that I appreciated it.

Although our expedition was fairly uneventful thereafter, I began to esteem all the work that went into creating a Sunday newspaper. And it meant nothing, none of it, if the package failed to be delivered.

Well, if lucky, I'll never forget any of that milestone morning—even before we hit the street. My big brother was already dressing by the blazing potbelly stove in the kitchen as my dad climbed the stairs to the unheated attic to awaken me. Oh, surely it broke his heart to rouse me from under that pile of blankets and coats, but nudge my shoulder he did.

And I answered my calling.

A Room of My Own

After coming home from a long morning in waiting rooms this day, I stepped inside our modest bungalow, threw my wife back in an effusive, manful embrace. Then withdrew to my study.

And there reflected: How favored I am to have a room of my own in which to retreat and do my writing. Virginia Woolf knew how essential that was, having published a whole book on the subject.

For nearly fifty years I've written for a living, but not until resigning from the fulltime newspaper timetable in '87 did I settle into a room of my own where I could do all my creative toiling.

Thus, inside these walls today, at my own pace, I find myself musing about the odd rooms where I've done time.

Right off, comes the oddest. 'Twas the night before I embarked on my newspaper career, ironically, that I moved into, a bedroom on the second floor of a Main Street funeral home in my new town, Blytheville, in the northeast tip of Arkansas.

My editor had rented the bedroom for me. Lodgings, he called it. When I braked my '49 Chevy at the address he'd jotted down, I knew he was only having a little fun with me.

But, no joke. That was it. A mortuary.

I went early to bed that night. It'd been a long haul from St. Louis, and I was expected on the job at 5:30 the next morning.

But not long afterward a scream shook me awake. I leapt from bed—I was just a pup of thirty-one then—and flung open the door, half expecting to see Miss Marple padding along the dim hall.

Then up the stairs came the sound of women weeping, followed by the deep chant of consoling voices. Naturally not all wakes in that funeral parlor were so dramatic, but that first one threw me for a loop. For an hour or so I lay awake out of sympathy for those poor folks downstairs.

However, the hardest thing to adjust to in that room over the next two years was the organ music, and you could expect it at any hour. When the chapel organist played, the walls throbbed, the windows rattled, the bed vibrated.

I'm not superstitious, but for some reason I could never put my clothes in the dresser drawers, and thus lived out of my footlocker, and the car trunk.

Obviously I didn't do much writing in that room of my own.

A reader might ask why I stayed so long. Well, it was clean, tastefully noncommittal, and the price right for an eager kid who came to work cheap as they come.

The chief drawback was no private entrance.

Often at night, or when I went home in the afternoon to sneak a nap between organ recitals, someone in a dark suit would get up from a chair, take my hand, and greet me with a mournful face.

"Friend of the family?" they'd say.

I made myriad friends in that mortuary where they'd put me to rest.

And from where I departed two years later on my own legs.

Super Bowl III—Plus One

Here's what I remember from the first Super Bowl I covered: riding to the game behind a police escort. Sirens bawling, bystanders rubbernecking—who could forget it?

The year: 1969. Game site: Miami's Orange Bowl.

Although I represented a clear international minority—a sportswriter who predicted a win for Joseph Namath's Jets over John Unitas's Colts—this had nothing to do with gaining preferential treatment en route to the contest. The exalted ride gyrated around the chutzpah of my friend and fellow writer from our newspaper's toy department.

We'd planned to meet in the lobby of the Miami Beach hotel that Sunday morning, then motor to the bowl in his automobile. As usual he was tardy.

Nervously I paced the lobby. Still, there were less impressive places to hang around waiting than the ritzy hotel, the NFL's bowl game headquarters. The lobby, as it had all week, buzzed with notables and hyperboles.

Not only was it my first Super Bowl. I was just a season removed from a beat in Blytheville, Arkansas, where the major sports unfolded on high school grids and courts. Now here I was talking and horsing around with living legends.

Brash broadcaster Howard Cosell created as much buzz as the players and coaches, cutting not quite a debonair figure as he stepped from the lobby elevator in shorts.

Finally my cohort from the newspaper emerged from an elevator, claiming he'd stayed up till all hours on that Super Bowl Eve tailing Namath, who, allegedly, had been whooping it up on the town. Even then my friend wasn't ready to head out, insisting on grabbing a bite of brunch at the NFL's expense. Not until czar Pete Rozelle left the hotel did we scramble for our car. My sidekick switched on his lights and brazenly hugged up to the rear of the commissioner's limo retinue, and off we wheeled through the traffic behind sirens and flashing reds and blues.

Of course there was no parking space reserved for us at the stadium, so we steered into a yard where a man waved a "pArK $5" sign.

By the time we unloaded our gear and went over to give the guy a fiver, the sign had cryptically changed to "pArK $10."

At the game I was assigned a cramped seat in front of the press penthouse, and at halftime I sullied my pants, trying to balance a box lunch and drink on my knees.

Truthfully, that's about all I recall of Super Bowl III. Yes, Namath lived up to his "guarantee"—and my prediction—of an upset of Baltimore, and yet it wasn't nearly as gratifying as my forecast of a win for a hometown team had been a few years before. Down by three touchdowns at the half, my boys had rallied to victory in a caterwauling rainstorm.

It's unlikely that any Super Bowlers will ever match that game for heart, titillation, and pure love of game.

And I had been there to record it from a rainswept press box, on a high school field in Arkansas. Where the parking was free.

April Foolery

Admirable restraint.

Yes, I believe these two words, though shopworn, correctly depict my recent utilization of journalistic judgment. I let another April Fools' Day march by without writing a column of buffoonery.

Almost all newspaper columnists at some point, usually at the sophomoric stage, write something outrageously unfounded on April first. It's a mortal temptation.

I fell to the bait in the mid-1950s while employed as sports editor on an Arkansas daily, in a town where a winning high school football season rated neck-and-neck with bumper crops of cotton and soybeans.

The school, pitiably, had suffered its first winless campaign ever. So, to jerk the townsfolk out of the dumps, I concocted a tongue-in-cheek yarn about a strapping newcomer who seemed a cinch to single-handedly turn next season into a winner.

What first caught the coach's eye, I wrote, was that the kid—and still just a ninth grader, mind you—came to school every morning swinging from tree to tree like Tarzan. I didn't pin a name on our super boy, but he was of Turkish descent, and his family lived east of town, so I labeled him the East End Bull.

Well, the writing of that cock-'n'-bull story proved a barrel of fun, and each year thereafter, as March ran out, I've had to stifle the hankering to crank out another prank.

Today most folks no longer have a distinctive approach to April Fools' Day. Dismally, many of these fictional yarns turn up more embarrassingly puerile than amusingly preposterous.

Another thing—some readers, in a hurry, might not

reach the bottom-line revelation that the author is merely April Fooling, and take the part they did read as gospel. It's not the purpose of newspapers to mislead readers. Honest. However, I still love the concept and potential of April Fools' Day and lament the paucity of the harmless elaborate joke or hoax.

We're a nation of needs these days, but none direr than some solid belly laughs.

Along about this time of year I feel a little guilty in this regard, that I didn't follow more faithfully in my dad's jaunty footsteps. In his blue Irish eyes, I think, most of life was a practical joke. At our house, Father's Day was April first.

Once, at the place where he worked in his last days, he placed a pair of shoes in the lone stall of the men's room, then arranged a pair of pants in elephant folds on top of the shoes where they could easily be seen under the swinging door. Before slipping back to work, he planted the final touch, an open vial of stink perfume. Can you imagine the fuss and frustration of the men who walked in and stormed out of the gents' as the day wore on?

At home that night, he laughed so hard trying to tell us about the repercussions of his ruse, he could hardly eat supper.

No fooling, my dad had the knack. I miss that. And him.

Hanging Out in America

I motored with one of our staff photographers a few years ago to southeast Florida to do a story. On the drive down, my sidekick, at the wheel, spied an image about a hundred yards off the road. With a yelp and a "look!" he slowed the car.

"Boy, wouldn't June go ape over that picture?"

June was a features writer at our newspaper, noted for her weakness for things woodsy, pastoral, and unfashionable.

Curiously, in a state bursting with enchantment for tourist and dweller alike, the rural picture that caught the lensman's eye that day was a single line of laundry, stretching from a neglected frame house to an unpainted, collapsing shed. What is there about a strand of laundry drying in the sun that stirs warm and homey passions in one's breast? Well, yes, it's a picture that almost everyone of a certain progressive age is inherently familiar with, and yet, now, a scene infrequently viewed on the national horizon.

Thus I shouldn't have been astonished, after writing a column recently about thunderstorms and laundry lines, that I heard from a galaxy of readers in whom nostalgic passions did deeply churn. One reader was carried back to the 1956 industrially charged East Chicago, Indiana, when he was a sassy fourteen-year-old helping "Busia," his Polish grandma, take down and shake her wash, griping about the "black grains" on her whites. In less than two sentences of broken English the grandma straightened him out, enlightening him about the "true value of that soot." Forty-six years later, as the reader poignantly observed, "it's all rust up there," and the men are looking for work. "Grandma was right."

Another reader reminisced about the only time he ever saw his mom cry, a Monday when a freakish wind upended the poles supporting her washlines, and cast her morning's work into the cinders in the yard. His boyhood home in Bellwood, Pennsylvania, was separated only by a dirt alley from the main line of the Pennsylvania Railroad. And he recalled that hoboes, hopping off boxcars, had his mom marked as an easy touch for meals and handouts. "I still miss her, thirty-two years after her death." Surely the hoboes do also.

Somewhere down the washline of time, half a century or so ago, the new-fangled automatic washers and dryers swept across this grand land of ours, symbolic of better economic days. Naturally not everyone was sold on them, but for so many individuals the acquisition of a new appliance was akin to stepping free of the Depression.

But the memories are there, more sweet than bitter, tidbit reminders of who we were, who we are, illustrations of Americana, faded but not vanquished.

I'd bet that at the very moment you're reading this, no matter the hour, there hangs a load of wash blowing in the wind.

And somewhere this winter there'll hang a lonely pair of men's BVDs frozen stiff on somebody's washline.

There's something touching about that.

Ah, Deadlines!

Newspapers are like jigsaw puzzles. They're put together piece by piece. And in the instance of daily journals, each interlocking piece, each department, has its own demanding deadline.

And so one lovely December day back in '86, confessing to myself that I no longer desired to play this demanding newspaper game, I signed up for retirement.

Naturally I had no illusions of retreating into a world unfettered by deadlines. Look around. They're all over the place.

Besides, before clearing out my desk and waving so long to that dexterous old gang of mine, I agreed to keep in touch by filing a weekly column from home.

I'm telling you, friends, you don't know what a deadline is until you've chased down a page-one story with only minutes to spare. And then there you are, ensconced at a keyboard, with the publisher, editor, and managing editor breathing hotly over your shoulder, waiting to see what blazing, factual revelations you're about to transmit to copy paper.

At the same time in another department of the plant, skilled pressmen are tinkering like railroad engineers with their oil cans, glancing anxiously at the clock, eager to throw the switch. You're also aware of the many delivery vehicles already lining up outside the building, waiting for your final touch to wrap up the day's product.

Now that's a headline of a deadline, take my word.

Old motion pictures lured me into the journalism trade at an early age. Seems I always had the yen to write, and I'd sit in the dark, spellbound by Hollywood's portrait of the big, busy, brassy newsroom—before computerization.

Ultimately, gratefully, I had my real-life share of it. Unfortunately, I missed the opportunity to imitate Clark Gable in that classic newsroom scene, the one where he yanks his story from the typewriter, waves it over his fedora and bellows, "Copy boy!"

That's OK. The newsroom dramatics fed all my expectations. Each day was Tchaikovsky's 1812 Overture all over again.

Late last Sunday afternoon, my wife, my in-house proofreader, appeared in my study. An editor had just called. Some redesigning was in the works, and could I possibly have my column in her hands by noon Monday? That'd be two days early. It also meant it should be in my wife's hands half an hour before noon, allotting her time to read and discuss my composition, then electronically route it into the newspaper's database downtown. The race was on.

I stayed plugged in at the keyboard until running out of gas.

Monday, fortified by sleep, breakfast, and shower, I dug in again. It'd been a long time since I'd written anything with one eye imperatively on the clock. Finally, 11:30 on the dot, bingo. I'd begun thinking I'd never hear the cannons go off again.

After throwing that last dot up on the display screen, I touched a few buttons. A disk popped out into my hand. I waved it overhead and I bellowed across the house, "Copy girl!"

Into That Corner of Panic

Funny thing happened to me while sitting here at the computer keyboard.

Suddenly I didn't know who I was.

There's more. I had no clue as to how I got here, or why.

This might sound like the opening chapter of a pulp whodunit, and admittedly it did leave me feeling creepy, but the segment was far from fiction.

Nor should anyone rush to assume that this recent incident surfaced as the direct result of symptoms commonly associated with advanced age. See, I actually knew who I was. That is, my name. Plus, I could reel off my Social Security digits. But the flesh and soul stuff was fuzzy.

You've likely experienced something similar yourself, haven't you, the chance to stand aside and look at the person you are, as other folks might observe you?

In my case, it wasn't quite as vivid as a scene played out in a film, with an actor standing to one side and squinting down at a dead-ringer of himself. No, it was hazier than that, and yet, at the same time, intensely demanding. So exacting, in fact, that I could feel myself backing into a corner of panic. And I considered slapping my face a few times—the way they used to do in the old Bette Davis movies—to snap myself out of it.

Was I losing my mind? Can't say. I've never lost my marbles before, so I've no concept as to what that condition feels like.

On a less flippant note, perhaps it had to do with peering too deeply into myself, afraid of finding out what's on the other side of my mind. I've skimmed that sort of introspection before. It's so easy to stand out there gaping at the moon until you lose your senses, but I've always known when to turn away, where to draw the line.

As I did this time, bringing myself back, luckily, to my study, my home, my spouse.

Putting it bluntly, the major headlines of the day do not make good reading. Seems awfully fitting, then, for one my age, or your age, to sporadically stand off, and listen to the rational voices of the past.

It's a funny world, folks, no joke. And apparently getting funnier by the day. Like it or not, it's ours.

This is awesome to contemplate, but we all have a turn at turning that world. Pray we get it right.

So maybe all this really does have to do with age: We are who we are, do what we do, at whatever age is ripe for us.

What I do know, sure enough, is this: The best time of day to check my own compass is when the curtain rings up on the morning. It's there and it's waiting to include me, the moment when I unseal the front door of our house, when I take my first sniff of the untouched day, when I take that first step outside into that gracious, understanding world of temporary sanity.

A Photo Op

Incredibly, not one person in the august assembly said to me, even in jest, "Are you going to put anything in the paper about us?"

This was a question routinely placed on my banquet plate when I was still actively out there on the circuit.

Circuit? Let me put it this way: back when I was still writing columns fulltime for my newspaper, and sifting inescapable invitations as an after-dinner orator.

Actually, harking back to the really old days—during the era when I was bearing up under my role as a get-up-and-go sports editor—the surest way for anyone to get a notice in my daily column was not to ask for it.

I recall the commander of an American Legion post inviting me to their hut for a catfish barbecue they were throwing that day, for their crackerjack baseball team. This was in Arkansas in 1959, my first newspaper job. I was the one-man sports department. I wrote the stories and head-lines, edited the wire copy, laid out each day's two or three pages, and snapped all the pictures with my faithful Speed Graphic.

"It's just an informal barbecue, a little show of appre-ciation for the boys," said the pooh-bah of American Legion Post 24, "and we'd like you to share it with us, ole buddy." Before hanging up he added, "Oh. Uh, don't forget to bring your camera."

Believe me, I've heard many variations of that theme, but here's the point. There were no such strings attached last week when my wife and I sat down to a luncheon with a company of retired military officers. That's why I'm eagerly tap-tap-tapping a few words on their behalf.

First, I did a three-year turn in the Army during World

War II, but I don't recall ever being surrounded by so much military brass as this. When I stepped up to spout a few words, I snapped off a salute to the naval commander who introduced me, and said, "Permission to board the dais, sir."

He snapped right back. "Permission granted."

I got a kick out of that exchange. Oddly, there was something of a back-home feel to it. But there was more. I felt surrounded by a warmth of men and women who'd been somewhere in this world and accomplished extraordinary deeds. I looked around the room and here's what I beheld: a cadre of bravery, sacrifice, and patriotic commitment.

I thanked these people, and prayed there are others of their stripe out there, younger for the most part, commanding and being commanded, able to put our world upright again. God bless 'em all.

Now, a final word on those 1959 Legionnaires. They were unable to pole enough catfish for their baseball team barbecue. Instead, they cooked up a huge crock of rabbit-squirrel-raccoon stew. First time I ever tasted anything of that sort, and it was superb.

Sorry, there are no photographic souvenirs of the event.

Mad Enough to Spit

Two men flew off the handle, and the game was cancelled in the top half of the first inning.

Too bad for the boys of the game, but a coach spat in the umpire's face. I no longer recall the play that triggered the tiff—not after thousands of play-by-plays. This I remember. I was covering sports for an Arkansas daily when this coach, from the Missouri Bootheel, led his American Legion baseball team south of the border to tan the hides of the local lads.

Before the game was a minute old, the visitor began riding the umpire from the first base coaching box. I felt compelled—nearly compelled—to trot over and notify him that the man behind the plate was an off-duty MP stationed at the nearby Air Force base. Plus, he had minor league experience with a rep for taking no guff from anybody. In a spring exhibition game in New Orleans he called out Ted Williams on strikes.

Actually, the coach should've guessed that here was not some backroad, run-of-the-mill, volunteer arbitrator. A big moose of a fellow he was, a voice to match, and on this sizzling day he showed up in a dark blue suit, little black cap and bow tie, and glossy black spikes.

In due course he commanded the coach to tone down the razzing, but the blowhard couldn't keep his lip zipped and was banished to the bench. And ultimately ordered off the grounds.

Oh, I'm telling you, that mulish coach was mad enough to spit. And spit he did.

While the rest of us on the set gasped, the Moose reacted with magisterial calm, snapping open a handkerchief and painstakingly wiping the spittle from his face. Next he waved his arms over his head and declared the game over and the home team the winner by forfeit.

The players—none older than seventeen—stood around blankly, watching the ump dump his gear in his car, change into civilian shoes, and after ankling over to the host coach to pick up his regular $5 work fee, drive off down the dusty road.

My guess, at that moment, the boys from Missouri had more respect for the umpire than for their own coach.

Ah, what a jolly good performance, and so said I in the newspaper the following day.

Umpires never see their names in the paper except in the fine-print boxscores, or unless hung up in a rhubarb. Theirs is not an easy lot. Anonymous underdogs, that's who they are. But essential Americans at the same time. Didn't a judge once rule that they couldn't strike because it'd be detrimental to America's favorite pastime?

Yep, sounds like a no-win situation.

And yet, forty years ago, I did see an ump win a game— and all by himself. Sometimes I think that's why I was in Arkansas on that day, to record the scene, give the Moose his due.

But even I've forgotten his real name.

You Don't Forget Jimmie Doolittle

My dad was in oil—a VIP with Shell Petroleum. And everybody in the neighborhood knew it.

Well, let me put it this way. Most everyone on our block and around our church parish was aware he worked for Shell in its own downtown St. Louis corporate office building. The VIP tag was a designation of my imagination.

At any rate, I did a double take at the recent newspaper headline proclaiming that the Shell service stations around Orlando are being swallowed up by Conoco. That's all I know about the deal, except that the familiar red and yellow symbol is ticketed for virtual extinction in these parts. What it means to the players in the world of high finance is beyond my scope. Most assuredly it doesn't affect me financially, for the only stock I have in Shell are blue-chip memories.

Shell became a household word around our old homestead. We had no automobile, but we simply knew Shell gas, in every respect, had it all over Texaco, Phillips 66, Sinclair, and the rest of the field.

I had no notion of how important Dad was in the structure of that mighty company, but they did hand him a weekly pay envelope throughout the Depression. Not until later years did I comprehend that the money they dispensed to him as a rate clerk was just barely enough for his family to squeak by on.

Not counting summertime, Dad wore a suit to work every day, and in the hot months he donned white shoes and straw hat—and always a tie, six days a week. Seven, if you count church.

As we sat down to supper one evening, he animatedly told about his meeting that day with a pilot on the Shell payroll, a prominent racer, a sparky guy by the name of Jimmie Doolittle. It's a name you don't forget.

Half a century later here in Florida, when the general and I were seated together at a banquet and I told him my dad had worked for Shell in St. Louis, he absolutely lit up.

"Ed Hayes? Oh sure, oh sure, I knew him well," and he raved on about my dad.

Of course the general, a recipient of the Medal of Honor, was only brimming over with blarney, God bless his soul, because the two had only met on the one occasion— and in the company restroom at that.

In 1942 when the war was only a few months old and looking bleak for the good guys, Doolittle had led a flight of B-52 bombers directly to Tokyo—the first raid on that city. Lord, what a brazen, morale-boosting move for our troops, as well as for their families at home. For my dad, with a son already in service and two more waiting to suit up, it was like a birthday gift. See, Doolittle staged his surprise party on April 18, 1942, and on that very same date forty-seven years before in Ireland, my dad was born.

I salute both my VIPs.

So Long, Enos

Early one winter's morn in 1955, I pulled open the main door of the newspaper office, cut through the uninhabited, unlit business department, and stepped into the cozy, well-lit editorial room. Freeing myself of my topcoat, I looked around for a closet, rack, or cupboard. The paper's editor, without a word, pointed to a stand that supported a bulging dictionary, so that's where I pitched the coat, and on that cavalier note, began my journalism days.

Scraps of foggy scenes and flimsy dialogue from that inaugural day intermittently float my way, but what's still fixed implacably in my memory is the first newspaper headline I ever wrote:

"Enos Balks At Wife No. 4."

Not unexpectedly, that headline again surfaced in my noggin a few days ago when the news services flashed word that Enos Slaughter, the North Carolina–bred baseball player who spent thirteen luminous seasons out in right field for the St. Louis Cardinals, had died at age eighty-six.

It seems well within the realm of irony that the Hall of Famer and I should hook up once more, forty-seven years after I parked at a newsroom desk the first time. And was assigned to write a one-line "head" on a dispatch hot off Associated Press' sportswire.

There I sat, a bit shaky, new job, new field, new town, and when I saw that it was a story about one of my favorite hometown baseball players, I surely must've snickered to myself. Like meeting an old sidekick, that's what it was—if only on paper.

The nub of the story: Slaughter was displeased about his divorce. Details, however, are irrelevant. The head I typed out on a slip of paper that morning was clever, I thought, and best of all, it fit the allotted space perfectly.

The sports editor of this small-city daily, whose job I'd be inheriting in a fortnight, glanced at the slip, then flicked it aside without as much as a mutter. Although I hadn't expected him to come galumphing around the desk to clap me on the back for my ingenuity and announce to the newsroom that a star was born, my hopes took a nosedive.

Maybe I was in the wrong line?

Ah, but when the edition clattered off the press that afternoon, there was my masterpiece, word for word, sticking out as if printed in cardinal-colored ink.

Back in my kiddie days, heroes never died. Everybody knew that. Slaughter, the strong-armed, hard-hitting, daring dynamo of the illustrious base paths, certainly fit the heroic cast for scores of little folks, and big people (sportswriters included), wherever baseball was played—and spoken.

True, he didn't issue from the same mold as, say, General Douglas MacArthur—the valorous old soldier who, in his own words, just faded away after World War II.

But our nation has always craved idols of assorted breeds.

And so I'm told that Enos Slaughter, another decorated hero, has died. I'm of an age now, unfortunately, where I believe that sort of thing.

Super Bowl Revisited

'Twas a long time ago that I last covered a Super Bowl.

Well, let's see, 1973, wasn't it?

Yes, it's all coming back now, the Miami Dolphins crowning a flawless season with a 14–7 decision over the Washington Redskins in the storied Los Angeles Coliseum.

Gosh, I was just a punk of forty-eight. A newspaper whippersnapper, you might say, and there I was, flying three thousand miles and bedding down in a ritzy hotel nestled in the middle of a golf course. It was such a swanky place, it almost made me forget that when our Orlando-to-L.A. aircraft stopped off in Dallas, somebody disembarked with my trenchcoat.

This was the year the National Football League staged its pre-game super soiree on the Queen Mary.

Imagine me, if you can, just a few years out of the Arkansas hinterlands, stepping aboard an ocean liner that night with all the NFL swells and big-name journalists.

Do you remember where you were on that Super Sunday in '73? Also feeling chipper and bushy-tailed, were you?

The first—and the only other—Super Bowl I worked gained renown as the contest in which Joe Namath "guaranteed" a victory for his upstart New York Jets over Johnny Unitas and his Baltimore Colts. For the record, I was one of the few sportswriters who took Broadway Joe at his word and backed him with a prediction of a win in print.

That was '69, in Miami. Ah, those were the heydays, my friends.

The Super Bowl was still something of a curiosity at the time. Even so, I went into the press area expecting too much. Why else was I less than impressed?

Perhaps, subconsciously, I was playing a game with myself, measuring the cream of the pros against the excitement of the high school boys from the Land of Opportunity.

And the Colts and Jets came up short. Honest.

OK, to be a little more specific about this, I moved from St. Louis, let's see, in '55 it was, to assume the sports editor's chair on a daily newspaper in Blytheville, Arkansas.

Several years later, on a dark and stormy night—I recall that well enough—the Hot Springs High School Trojans rolled into town and mopped up the Blytheville High Chickasaws in the first half. Down 19–0, it took some true grit for the Chicks to hit that yucky field after intermission—and for the spectators to stick around. Rain and tears streaming down their faces, the fans saw the mud-shrouded hometown boys pull off the impossible. They bared their hearts and they barred the visitors from scoring again, meantime posting three touchdowns of their own, unbelievably, and enough extra points, unimaginably, to win.

The tingle of it for me was going back to the empty newspaper office that night, and sitting at the typewriter to tell my readers all about it.

And somehow feeling that it was never again going to be this good.

How wrong I was. Here I am doing it again.

'Tis the Season

We Were That Class

How peculiar it always seemed, sitting down at my schooldesk again after returning from the year-end holidays.

It'd only been a week or so—compared to the meandering three months of summer vacations—and yet everything felt so different, so foreign.

For one thing, Christmas had happened. My classmates and I, one more time, had climbed the vast spiritual and commercial mountain.

Something else. A new calendar hung on the wall up front and suddenly each boy and girl in that school, without exception, was a year older. And wiser, of course. That's the January of my memory.

I can also see a kid coming out the front double doors on the last day of school before one of those peerless Christmas breaks, and calling to a mate across the icy street, "Hey, Leonard! See you next year, pal!" That struck me as a snappy phrase, one that I might wriggle into a conversation at home, possibly just before going up to bed on New Year's Eve. "See you next year, Dad!" If ever it came about that I did indeed voice those words, I can't honestly say. That was long ago—back in the days when it was a strain to stay awake until twelve midnight, despite my honorable intentions.

Realistically, it hasn't been so terribly long ago that it required abundant effort to keep my eyes wide open on New Year's Eve. Last year, in fact. This year, no problem at all. This year at the venerable stroke of midnight, my wife and I happened to be doing up the twin beds in the guest bedroom—for ourselves. One of the two heating units at our place, you see, fizzled out. *Pffft!* Just like that. No advance notice. How rude. In quick time, sections of our lodgings, including the mistress/master bedroom, covered over with frost.

Sure, we felt put out, who wouldn't, but how much better off we were, for example, than the hordes of red-eyed, weather-stranded travelers out at Orlando International Airport on that same hallowed night.

Lord, how overwhelming it all seems now, the whole, bursting bag of life, as I glance back from that night of the New Year 2001, to one of the days in the old 1930s, another January, where I try fitting back into the ranks at school.

Seated, encircled by shiny, cold-tinted faces, I find it easy to pick out the Christmas presents, the radiant new sweaters and socks, a snappy pair of red suspenders, the fountain pens, and fancy hair clips.

One boy admires his new wristwatch so often, the teacher asks him if he has a train to catch.

And the room fairly sparkles with colorful new ties, the ubiquitous, grudgingly appreciated Christmas gift.

Ties, and shirts and skirts, were the strict regulation of the day.

For most of us little people sitting in that enshrined classroom, it was going to be a long haul, but we were all dressed up and ready to go.

What a Little Paint Can Do

Long have I fancied the skill of those who do splendid things with paintbrushes.

I stand to the side, the observer, green with envy, as they create landscapes and portraits on canvas, as they daub flagpoles and fences, and—to add a note of relevance—as they stroke residential interiors back to life.

As a reader might suppose, my wife and I are currently having the inside of our little domicile painted. Although the painter's end of the project is technically complete, we've still not settled back into all of our familiar pockets.

Homeowners who've been through this—shifting furniture and utensils and personal belongings around and about—know what I'm talking about. Automatically you reach out for an object in its fixed position, and it's not there. Or brush lightly against a desk to guide you toward the bathroom during the night, and you can't feel it. Sure you're in the right house, old boy?

The other morning, aghast, I snapped on the bathroom light, and instead of seeing my face in the mirror, I stared into a rectangular hole the size of a medicine chest, filled with bricks and mortar.

One of these days we might be able to walk from room to room without having to pick a path through the jungle of books. Presently I'm not at all convinced that every last volume will fit on the bookshelves from whence they came. Overnight they've proliferated. We've already weeded out more than a hundred, destined to get back into circulation through the stalls of the public library's used book store.

Our place has needed fresh makeup for quite a spell, and when our hired hand called to say he'd be available the next morning, we flashed the green light and cancelled all dates.

Either that or do the job ourselves. Although I've been retired long enough to have learned another trade, I still can't make magical moves with a brush.

Like all painters—whether they paint a portrait or the broad side of a barn—our chosen one is an artist, swift and sure. Best of all he has the decency to listen to his music via headset.

I've always thought workmen made their own luncheon deals. What's the protocol? When our man showed no sign of taking a noontime break, were my wife and I supposed to sit at the table and try to enjoy a guilt-free repast—under his eyes?

Finally I spoke up: "Uh, care to join us?" Unhesitatingly: "Yes."

And so for two weeks he sat with us on the deck each noon for a sandwich, soup, fruit, and a share of our pot of tea.

In addition to weeding our bookshelves, I gave my desk drawers and files a thorough, tough purging, finally admitting that some of my golden manuscripts were never going to be sent anywhere except the city dump.

I feel pounds lighter. Fresh and clean. Just like the house. A splendid, honest way to start a new year.

Happy New Face!

Did you ever look at your face in the mirror, and stretch the skin back tautly from beneath each ear?

Tell the truth.

If yes, did you lo-and-*behold!* the disappearance of certain wrinkles and crevices carved by Father Time? Did you like what you saw, the picture of yourself as the world viewed you a few years ago?

Or maybe your face doesn't reveal such telltale clues. Lucky you.

These questions, essentially, were contrived for the older blokes in the audience, men and women my age, retirement age, give or take a handful of years. However, I reckon, they could be put to individuals of almost any span, depending on one's outlook and vanity. Just as vanity is a reality of life, so it is that we don't all start showing up old according to the same timetable.

Not long ago, a dear friend of mine whose reputation as a straight shooter is legendary, casually remarked, "You always look the same."

That could be taken as a compliment, except in my case I began looking old long before my time. It's true. I'm not fishing for phony tributes.

Be that as it may, as they say, I looked at my face in the mirror this morning prior to the daily ritual of shaving— that splendid, inalienable rite of manhood—and decided to give myself the old do-it-yourself facial surgery test. It was probably prompted by something my wife said.

"I think," said she, "you should let me trim that hair over your ears."

I said, "Oh, I don't mind looking a little craggy." I was thinking of craggily handsome, without actually saying it.

But then she said, "It makes you look old." That did it.

Ever since my woman took over as my hairdresser, she's been trying to keep me neatly pruned, a look that hasn't altogether met with favor among all my relatives.

Well, it was my younger brother's spouse who came right out with it, saying she preferred my previous shaggier mane because "it made you look like Mark Twain."

Again the earmarks of a compliment—except that in the only pictures of Twain around this house, he looks like he's in the death grip of the old-timer with the scythe and hourglass who makes a doddering appearance at the close of the year.

Hence, I grant my barber free reign with the scissors.

Speaking of look-alikes. Do people ever remark that you resemble a certain prominent personality? Does the allusion please you?

OK, back to the bathroom mirror. I stretched my facial hide, and the old tracks did indeed vanish. Wait, on closer inspection, it gave me a pasty, unnatural look. It wasn't me. So I've decided to save face, that's it, keep the one I have, for better or for worse for wear.

I think we're all who we are, hour by hour, day by day, and that's that.

Now let's go out and put on a Happy-New-Year face.

A Ladies' Man

As far back as I can remember, and probably farther beyond than that, February has stretched across my imagination as an enormous wasteland.

If it hadn't been for two dates on the calendar, a pair of oases, especially in my chipper days, I wouldn't have minded skipping the month altogether.

The first was February ninth—my older brother's birthday. It came hopping along just in the nick, tailor-made to rescue a jaded wayfarer from the doldrums that so often ride the flagging coattails of Christmas, New Year's Eve, and jolly January itself.

Where I come from, the Midwest, February was a sort of weak sister—if one might still use that analogy. The weather was iffy, seldom nifty, but who cared when it came time to salute the birthday boy?

The birthday boy turned eighty-one this year.

Holy mackerel, I well remember when he only had to blow out five or six candles, or a mere dozen. A cute little guy, I guess, something of a cutup he was, and a little bossy with his two little brothers; but that's the way it goes with trailblazing big brothers. Big sisters too, I have the feeling. They're nothing if wishy-washy.

I *loved* that boy.

In those scrimpy days we had no lavish birthday parties to include the whole neighborhood gang, although two cousins would usually drop around on the way home from school and join us for indoor games and cake.

Two-layer cakes were OK for Sundays, but no matter how much money we had on hand or didn't have, Mom always managed to turn out a picture-perfect, taste-perfect, three-layer cake from her special-events oven.

And then, before we knew it, February fourteenth was on the doorstep, St. Valentine's Day, another nice little boost before entrenching for the dragging, cold academic campaign toward Easter.

I always regarded my dad as a romantic. I do believe he shone brightest when in the company of women. And yet I can't ever recall him giving our mom a valentine or a gift of any kind on that hallowed day. My guess would be that he assuredly did so during his courting days, but after the wedding, things got a little complicated, the way they do.

Of course, for all I know, when Dad realized he could afford to make the payments on a new refrigerator and get rid of our old wooden icebox, *that* could very well have been a truly worthy valentine for his spouse.

The only gifts we boys looked for on that day were chocolate kisses and heart-shaped redhots. Oh, and the valentines. After doing the supper dishes we'd sit around the table, showing off the valentines we got in school. Big brother always amassed the most. Like our dad, he was a ladies' man.

And now he's the elder of the clan. I think maybe Mom and Dad might be smiling down, knowing they left us in good hands.

I still love that boy.

My Dad Himself

My dad never asked for much in his lifetime, and demanded even less.

One matter he was strict about, however. Whether St. Patrick's Day or any other calendar day, he didn't want anybody fiddling with his brew. Such as? Slipping a green food-coloring pellet in his glass, for instance.

Some merrymakers do pull these sorts of tricks in their zeal to celebrate the revered one's birthday—St. Patrick's, that is, not my dad's—maybe whipping up a bowl of green mashed potatoes, and so on.

However, himself, my dad, had his limits.

Naturally he didn't mind if my mom, sporting a green ribbon in her hair, surprised us by carrying an all-green, fresh-baked layer cake to the supper table on March seventeenth—following the main course of boiled corned beef, cabbage, and spuds.

But the whole idea of him sitting down after supper and sipping a glass of *green* beer, while reading the newspaper or listening to the radio, was totally revolting. I think it would've been like me trying to down a tumbler of green milk, or pouring ghastly green gravy over Mom's celebrated, breaded veal cutlets.

Ordinarily I find the color green rather pleasant, but I too have my statute of limitations, including green socks, and boxer shorts with shamrocks imprinted thereon.

Dad was born in Ireland, but he was an American by choice and by formal declaration. Quietly—for that's the brand of man he truly was—he swung aboard a St. Louis streetcar one morning and came back home that evening a citizen of these United States.

Official immigration records confirm that Dad, a

native of County Clare on the Emerald Isle, landed at Ellis Island on the seventeenth day of September, the year 1916, at the tender age of twenty-one.

Often I think of him on his Atlantic-tossed ship, the *St. Paul,* and him no doubt realizing deep in his heart that he would never again set eye on his parents. He knew not a soul in this rambling country save for an older brother, a priest, who died shortly thereafter. And then indeed he was on his own, an ocean from home.

My dad was no hero, although it's a snap for me to cast him in that role, sailing to this country on nothing but a prayer and a brogue. But countless thousands, yea millions, before and after him were in the same boat, all part of the great American symphony.

They toiled, obeyed the laws, pledged allegiance to the flag, married, voted, and served on juries. My dad never earned a million bucks in his brief sixty-two years, never wrote a poem or drove a car, or had a checking account, but you know what? He did have a devoted wife and three sons who loved, honored, and obeyed him.

I've been thinking, what this disjointed world needs is another St. Patrick. Something else. Maybe it could also use another Edward Francis Hayes.

That's my dad.

Once Upon an Easter

*O*nce upon an *E*aster time there were three
little boys standing by the round table in the cozy kitchen
of a small frame house. On the table were a dozen or so
boiled eggs. Also standing in a nearby row were seven or
eight cups, each one brimming with warm water of a different vivid color.

'Twas the morning before Easter Sunday.

Now, if you take a closer look at this picture, and
swear that the boy in the center—the middle son, the cute
one with dark brown hair and a shy smile—resembles me,
you'd be right on the nose.

The precise year of this diaphanous snapshot isn't clear,
although it's clear enough that we lads were still serving time
in the local grammar school. But I feel quite sure that this was
the first time the three of us were allowed to take an active
part in the grandiose production of coloring our own Easter
eggs.

Before then, it was common knowledge that those
dyed, eye-catching, edible nuggets were delivered to the
homes of good little boys and girls by the Easter Bunny
himself.

Anyway, now that the secret was out, my older brother was despoiled of his standard Easter morning routine. At
the back window he'd cry, "Look, there goes the Easter
Rabbit!" Oh, sure, and by the time my little brother and I,
exhilarated, had barefooted across to verify the rare
appearance, the yard would be empty, and the big boy
would say, "Aw, gee, guys, he just jumped over the hedge,"
or conciliatory words to that straight-faced effect.

How many years did we fall for that performance anyway? At any count, nearly seventy years have passed since

the aforementioned snapshot was filed in my memory.

And the three little boys in the picture? We're still around, thank the Lord.

Now and again when I treat my wife to lunch downtown, we pay a social call afterward to my little brother at his work place. On our last visit, several days ago, the main subject was his retirement.

And so it has come to pass, after all this time, after the years of schooling and the wearing of wartime uniforms, and laboring long in the vineyard, falling in love, and accumulating families, the siblings are united in still another brotherhood: voluntary retirement.

My kid brother's final days on the regular work force have narrowed down to this week, Easter week. And an apt choice I'd say: the dawn of a new vision, his own resurrection, if you will.

It's been a long, godsend of a haul.

Oh, yes, there was more to Easter than stuffing baskets with fake grass, chocolates, and sweet debris.

At church there was a special feature every day in the week leading up to the big day, and you better believe Mom made sure her little ones were in the pews.

The ancient snapshot of us standing in the kitchen hasn't faded. A family that colors eggs together stays together.

Happy Godfather's Day

If it hadn't been for his family, I believe my dad would've been content to be one of life's silent partners, to tiptoe along without anyone paying any attention to him.

Once upon a time he was a young man of average height, above average in looks, and fresh off the boat from Ireland. Some of the native fellas found his clothes and his brogue funny, but in hardly any time at all he became a quiet part of the streaming American scene. He found work in a shoe factory, and there met Julius, a strapping fella of German stock who became his lifelong friend.

And post-lifetime friend, I pray.

For a time they went off on separate tracks as my dad shifted to a more suitable job, in the accounting department of a railroad company. There, in his new setting, the Irish boy caught the eye of a budding, bespectacled Bohemian-American girl. Ah, a diligent clerk with dark, darting eyes named Anna.

And so as young people then were wont to say, he began to seriously court Anna, the tall, timorous flower who was to become my mom. In hardly any time at all thereafter, the two lovebirds exchanged vows in her family's parish church; and my dad's hope of leading a quiet, anonymous life began dissolving.

He sired three sons, all of whom were destined to make some noise in this world.

I, the middle son, came along in the summer of '24.

And it was good old Julius, chosen to be my godfather, who held me in his arms at the baptismal font. How unfortunate it is that the word godfather itself, in recent years, has fallen into comic-tragic reference. How could a title so spiritually honorable be awarded to a crime czar?

Julius shouldered his new role religiously. Because he knew my dad so well, it seems doubtful that he fretted much about my losing the faith, and yet throughout my childhood he stayed in touch. A bachelor who supported his two maiden sisters, Julius boarded a streetcar for the half-hour's trip to our house no less than once a month. On these visits he'd lay his mammoth hand on my head, and press a quarter into my palm. If my brothers—and maybe a cousin—were on the premises, they'd each pocket a dime. Once behind our backs, he paid a neighborhood merchant to deliver a bulging basket of groceries to our doorstep.

Always on his visits to our house, Mom served a light lunch, which included a wedge of malodorous Limburger cheese that Julius relished. It was the only thing I ever held against him.

For me, Father's Day is also thanksgiving day. How lucky I was, born in a home with a live-in father. Not only that, quietly and lovingly, he knew I was there. Not only *that,* I was blessed with an honest-to-goodness godfather.

Happy Father's Day to them both.

And the same to all daddies and goddaddies here and thereafter.

Psst! Happy Birthday!

It's unlikely I could come even close to guessing the number of times I've sung the "Happy Birthday to You" song.

Or, come to that, played the ditty on my fiddle in someone's honor.

Close to one thousand all told? Give or take, it's still a merry idea to play with, if one takes the time, particularly as each rendition surely reflects a gem of a moment from the past.

How about your gems? Wouldn't you like to see again the mirror of that first birthday candle in the eyes of your first child, or the flood of light on a parent's or grandparent's last birthday cake, while hearing the stout echoes of "Happy Birthday"?

I can't name any other song that makes even my tone-deaf relatives believe they can outdo Pavarotti.

Also, it'd be just another wild guess trying to determine the amount of occasions when I've added my voice and violin bow to the glad tidings of "Happy Birthday to You" in *public*.

In short, how often I've performed the song illegally.

What's that? That's right. I don't mean to throw a wet blanket on your sentimental journey, but the song is copyrighted, and if ever you performed it in public without paying royalties, or obtaining permission, you stand guilty.

I thought I'd learned all the facts of life years ago, but evidently this one escaped me until a recent Sunday, when, after breakfast, the owner of the restaurant showed me a newspaper clipping someone had sent to him. The headline: "Singing 'Happy Birthday' could cost you $10,000."

So *that's* why I've never heard it sung in my friend's

eatery. He might send a surprise ice cream spectacular over to the table, but never a warbling waitress. Smart cookie.

You'd think that after all these years the song would be fair game for the populace. True, the tune was composed a hundred years ago—by two Louisville school teachers, sisters Patty and Mildred Hill—but with the words "Good Morning to You."

That's correct. The "Happy Birthday" lyrics weren't coupled to the melody until republished thirty-five years later. And that's the piece that remains sealed by copyright until 2010.

While emphatically applauding protection for artists' work in all forms, I do question how far the long arm of the law can reach before sinking to the tier of tomfoolery.

But it's no joke, as the news clip states, "to the agents who scour the U.S.A., popping up unexpectedly in restaurants, nightclubs, bars, and even summer camps, looking for lawbreakers."

Summer camps? Picture it on the evening news: a troop of Boy Scouts nabbed in the act of singing "Happy Birthday to You" while gathered around a campfire, and hauled off ignominiously to court.

To play it sensibly, then, we should probably confine our renderings of "Happy Birthday" to the home—until, optimistically, 2010.

Meantime, if today happens to be the birthday of anyone reading these words, here's hoping that he or she will take the following message personally.

"Happy birthday, dear reader, happy birthday to you!"
You know the melody.

Mirror, Mirror

In my older brother's letter—flown in to Orlando from St. Louis—he reminded me that Flag Day was upcoming. He's a fine one, indeed, when it comes to prompting me about approaching birthdays, anniversaries, the odd holiday, and other celebrations.

So there I was on Flag Day morn, planting a couple of small United States of America flags—on sticks about a yardstick high—at the edge of the road, one on each side of our gravel driveway.

I fostered no hope that my newspaper would assign a photographer to record this patriotic display, or that television crews and their trucks would soon be in command of our quiet, dead-end road. Even so, the modest exhibit, I must say, did look quite stirring in the rippling, freckled sunlight.

Hours later when I went out in the gloaming to collect my flags—now get this—they had *disappeared!* How could that be? I checked with my wife. Had she rounded them up for me, stored them in the shed? Sorry, no, said she.

Ladies and gentlemen, somebody had the blasphemous gall to swipe our flags. In broad daylight, mind you. Right under the nose of a World War II veteran who logged two years out there in the not-so-pacific South Pacific. What was our world coming to?

Understand, I didn't feel violated, or financially wounded, or anything of the sort. Regardless, I did stand there empty-handed, looking up and down the road with a rising sense of slight amusement, which gave way, bit by bit, to bafflement and vulnerability.

Were prankish kids the culprits? Maybe hardened crooks? Hardened Communists?

Should I dial 911? The Military Police?

Suddenly I was reminded of my friend Pete who dwells a couple of miles from here. He flew bombers during the war, and not long ago this decorated colonel suffered the ignominy of having three flags stolen from the pole in front of his house—on three successive holidays. What kind of respect is that?

Now with the Fourth of July coming up, should I invest in two more flags? If so, do I squat behind the bushes and wait for the flag swiper to strike again? What kind of Independence Day is that?

All right, so moving right along to another matter—to the next day after all these flag hi-jinks—my wife decided to remove a mirror, recently cracked by a workman, from our premises. Hanging near the door leading to the sundeck, it was a big congenial mirror, bordered with splashes of brightly painted flowers that opened up the wall like a window. She replaced the mirror with a glass-framed painting, and in general prettied up the corner.

That evening, after toting a full bag of garbage out to the road for the usual early-morning pickup, I propped the mirror against it. Half an hour later I ambled out in the dark to stuff some overlooked scraps into the garbage bag.

The mirror had vanished.

The Summers We Stayed Home

"Going anywhere on vacation this summer?"
Often when dealing with this predictable question, I ponder—and sometimes mumble ever so engagingly to myself—about how profoundly endowed we citizens of this country be. Well, if only for the simple fact of taking it for granted that almost everyone we know has the *means* to go juttering off on vacation. Plus the opportunity to do so.

This isn't Belfast or Kashmir, where the word vacation is often translated into two sides agreeing to a temporary cessation of warfare. We don't live in Serajevo or Jerusalem, one of those cities of long goodbyes, where the odds of getting to work and back, or making a safe roundtrip to fetch a loaf of bread, are fifty-fifty at best.

Thank goodness we can reserve our ceremonious goodbyes for cruises and flights and lengthy highway hauls, or at least until—if ever—the bloodthirsty screwballs of the universe gain the upper hand.

Over the years, I've rarely experienced the craving to go off somewhere on vacation. Perhaps the adventures of World War II squelched my wanderlust. Which is not to imply that I wouldn't pack up my old kit bag this very day if an impossible-to-refuse possibility came bounding my way.

Naturally there are some individuals who inaccurately suspect I've been on a perpetual vacation the last fifteen years upon signing up for monthly Social Security checks. For the sake of honest bookkeeping, be it noted that not one week has gone by, dating back to '87, that I've not faced a newspaper deadline. But that's my option.

Regardless, I can only guess how spectacular it must've felt, in whatever grade-school classroom I happened to be at the time, when it dawned on me what the word vacation was all about. No schoolwork, no homework for three months running? Too numbing, surely, for a mere grammar schooler to comprehend.

Possibly because of the Depression, scarcely anyone in our circle gave thought to going away for a vacation, and that was OK with me. After chores and running errands, the hours belonged to us, the girls and boys of summer, to romp, to daydream. Nothing was out of bounds.

I do recall the summer of '34, I was ten, when the family of five next door drove in their jalopy, St. Louis to California, to visit relatives. Gone about a month. How strange it stood, the house, dark, stark, and void for so long.

Then one day I heard the jubilant horn of their returning car, honking nonstop from the far end of the alley till they pulled up at their garage—the neighborhood ticking again.

Labor Day arrived soon thereafter, vacation over, and we were trekking back to school, and passing no armed soldiers along the way, everybody a wee bit older.

Halloween was the next bright light up ahead, but it was still a long, long way to Thanksgiving, to Christmas.

You remember those days yourself, don't you, the days we thought would never get here?

Dressed to Kill

Fourth of July is a snappy salute to a group of colonists who dared to be dazzling. It's a celebration of our first reveille, a sonnet to apple pie, potato salad, independence, hot dogs, baked beans, freedom, fireworks, patriotic merrymaking, picnics, and paper plates.

OK, but whatever happened to picnic pants? Are sailors the only ones wearing white pants any more?

Sure, some white pants are surely worn by *some* civilians, but along the social scenes of my everyday scrutiny they're not what you might classify as a high-fashion item.

Sunday morning in church, I looked around. Not a single pair of white ducks in evidence, and once upon a time they were the flags of summer. Long ago when a fellow hitched up a pair of white pants, and topped it with a dark blue sports coat, and went ankling down the avenue to pick up his girl, people sitting out on porches would nod to one another.

"Dressed to kill," they'd say admiringly. How or why that old expression came in to play I can't say, but in our rambunctious society today it's probably best not to pursue the issue.

What I did see in church were youngsters sporting expensive, bizarre-hued, unpressed, sagging, baggy pants. And for some reason these fashion mavens seemed to have difficulty standing without the balance of hands buried in their pockets. Not one pair of prayerfully folded hands in evidence.

I recall the prideful wearing of sailor pants, or picnic pants, as a boy on Independence Day outings. Almost every lad, even from poor families like ours, had a pair washed and ironed and ready for dressing up—and especially for the annual school picnic.

Boy, those picnics. Remember? How great they were.

At our school each grade was assigned to a double-decker bus that carried us to the amusement park on a bluff overlooking the Mississippi River. We'd hit the gravel-covered grounds in stampede, sprinting for the Dodge 'Em, Pretzel, Crazy House, Ferris Wheel, and that stupendous Penny Arcade. Moms staked out picnic tables with their lunch baskets in the pavilion, preferably as far away from the headache-inducing, screaming roller coaster as possible.

Picnic pants and skirts didn't stay immaculate, but at day's end they bore the happy smudges of childhood's splendid freedom. Alas, a few years later, it was on to World War II and my dream of wearing a Navy uniform like my older brother. But when conscription came breathing down my neck, the general opinion around our household was that those skin-tight, bellbottom pants would do little to flatter my tall, skinny, gawky silhouette. It's doubtful the Army uniform did anything for me, either, but I rode out the war in khaki and color-coordinated fatigues.

Possibly one good reason we no longer see much of picnic pants is that a number of folks share my problem. Fifty years and a few too *many* pounds later, I still don't have the figure to wear a pair.

Write Your Own Saga

I was thinking about you this morning. It's true. And thinking I'd open this essay by asking if you'd checked your calendar yet. Next I would remind you that another August was on the brink of dropping its curtain.

But at that point, something tripped in my brain, and I went back for a closer look at two key words: Another August. And said to myself, "Hmmm, that wouldn't make a bad book title."

OK, so let's take a look at that.

"*Another August,*" as the dust-jacket blurb might blurt, "is the raw, gripping story of an older Renaissance man finally coming to grips with himself, after a peripatetic life packed with tempestuous loves and other impassioned imbroglios, set against a flaming tapestry of hurricanes and of global war and peace."

The beauty of the title, *Another August,* you see, is that it fits the life story of just about any man or woman, not mine alone.

Oh, yes, you and I, we all have our stories to spin. It's doubtful there is one character among us—rich man, poor man, beggar man, politician—who doesn't believe that his or her own life has all the chewy stuff, who doesn't dream that it would positively make a *Moby Dick* of a book—if written.

I found out something along those distressing lines, back in the days while serving my newspaper as book editor. And, for some wayward reason, a myriad of these aspiring autobiographers approached me with offers to write their intriguing, inspirational life epics for them. Some were quite magnanimous about it, offering me nice little percentages of the profits if and when the volumes were published and, of course, converted into motion pictures.

At any rate, August, the month, is the metaphor in the case at hand. As we all know, no self-respecting book would dare show its face without at least one good metaphor. In a nutshell, then, August is the dramatic bridge between the long haul of summer and the pleasant promises of autumn.

And, if I may be allowed to interject another literary reminder, it was William Faulkner who achieved immortality by writing of the bridges of Yoknapatawpha County. All right, maybe our lives are not as convoluted as Faulkner's dark yarns, but I think all of us, young, old, and in between, walk the bridges to crucial decisions. Whether they be as simple as thinking things over, putting our lives into meaningful perspective. Whether we dream of publishing our sagas or not.

You know, I rather like the changes of seasons.

Assuredly I look upon the gradual and sensual alterations of the trees and foliage as my own treasure island, although it also becomes a time for emotional reorganization.

And so, here we are, review time, the end of another August. Time to make amends, meet our own expectations, and maybe work up a resolution or two.

Time to step off into what will be—with a little luck—the winter of content.

And Get Back Safely

Are you going to have a big Labor Day?
Precisely what that question implies, I'm not sure. Even so, it's one I often heard while still a member in good standing of the punch-clock labor force, and remember yet, a decade or so into the retirement force.

It was not a question reserved exclusively for Labor Day. Copious, too, were the times fellow workers inquired if I was going to have a big Christmas, a big Fourth, a big Easter.

Lovely of them to ask, of course.

The thought crosses my mind today that I was endowed with a quantity of unselfish, caring coworkers in my days of the weekly paycheck. Fortunately, the handful of faces in my rogues' gallery is fast fading.

Unfortunately, many men and women measure their laboring days from one holiday to another. Pity, that. From my first step into a newspaper office in 1955, I anticipated with relish every working day that flung open its welcoming arms.

Before that date, before opening the door and taking my seat behind a typewriter, the labor course was far less compensatory. That's where young folks aplenty are presently stuck. Many of us were so mired. But each step led us to being the individuals we are today, whatever we might be doing.

I slung my share of milk and beer bottles, nuts and bolts, bread and freight in factories and on loading docks, but I knew—felt fairly cocky about it, in any event—that my time would come.

Say, if you find yourself gladly reporting for duty at five o'clock on a Monday morning—as I did for twenty years—

you know you're home.

A big holiday, eh? What's that mean? A big shindig? A gang of people aboard, nonstop sound effects, abundant food and drink?

I've never been much of a shindig person. Tranquility's my game. Well, yes, certainly I cherish the coming and going of family and friends at events like Thanksgiving, succulence on the table, laughter on the wing, the piano getting a voracious workout. Christmastime, too, when the rooms are never big enough to hold all the traffic and trappings.

When associates ask if you're going to have a big holiday, what they're really doing, I think, is wishing you bon voyage, that the time will turn out to be all you expected of it. In the end, it means returning safely.

For me, in past years, Labor Day arrived with a touch of remorse, marking completion of the long summer, the shutdown of amusement parks and swimming pools, storing straw hats and white shoes, and the unlocking of the schoolhouse doors.

I still can't get accustomed to children attending classes in August, but don't mind me. It'll work out. All of this will eventually be somebody else's fond memory.

Life ticks on and on. One day you're part of the work force, and before you know it, if you're lucky, every day is a paid holiday.

Whatever Labor Day means to you, have a big one.

Labor Day's Own Sweet Song

September sings its own song.

The tune is familiar, one year after another, a shade of wistfulness at the start, then a heavy touch of unwillingness to move on down the line.

How much summer can young people—the occupants with the most to lose—pack into the last sweet, frantic days of August?

For the others, the individuals sporting visible emblems of age and wisdom, September is more than another season; it rises up formally, not unlike another new year. Little wonder the years get here so quickly.

Back yonder, under the temporary guise of a boy, I watched Labor Days come and I watched them slip away, and when the frolic of the day was spent, the public swimming pool officially shut down. A sad, sad day it was, the day after, the pool drained, the gate padlocked, but still audible the wondrous splash and cry. It was also the day my dad put away his straw hat, sealed it in a wrinkled shopping bag, tucked it in a closet corner.

True, there would be a hot day up ahead when he wished he hadn't packed it, and then another, or wished he could still wear his white shoes and seersucker pants to work, but he played by fashion's emblazoned, seasonal rules.

Those same unspoken policies dictated that my mom wear gloves to church, also when boarding a streetcar or a bus.

Then the boys and girls coming together, neckties and shiny shoes and pretty pleated skirts, thin voices lifted, another movement of September's serenade. From every direction the students connected, crossing quiet streets and skipping along flurried sidewalks, all the gang converging on the schoolyard, and smelling of sun and watermelons. Reunions all over the place.

And there, at the link fence, the bashful boy, his eyes searching the yard for the comeliest girl of them all, afraid she hadn't come back this time, and then afraid to open his mouth once he picks her out. A whole lifetime will go by without ever uttering a word to her about this sterling instant, or about anything else.

Now the hammer rattles the bell, the nine o'clock alarm, the summer is over. The yard clears; the last syllable of jabberwocky vanishes.

Only the young can leave this kind of silence behind, deep as unending sleep.

And the nervous neighborhood dogs trot back to their naps.

September is the saga of scents of unbroken chalk and clean erasers, of lunch boxes, of pungent new books, and soon our albums fill with pictures of the Depression, of war, peace, farewells, marriage, and childbirth.

September is yesterday and today and tomorrow. Each September brings somebody new into the scene, and we're all in it together, sharing these thoughts, now, this instant, at the breakfast table, in a sick bed, waiting for a flight at the airport.

If you don't know the words of the song, it's all right. The greatest lyrics, the hopes, are unspoken anyway.

It's September. Come hum along.

Moonlight Sonnet

In the middle of the night, during the full-moon cycle, I rise up from bed and feel my way, squinty-eyed, through two rooms. Not until reaching the bathroom—the location I visit periodically during my sleep cycles just to make sure everything in there is copacetic—do I realize I need not have made the trip by memory.

Raw, silver moonlight, unbroken by the window's frosted glass, swabs my eyes and swamps the bathroom and dazzles against the white tile of the floor and walls.

Back once more in the bedroom, I'm tempted to fetch the mystery novel from my bedside table, sit in the wicker chair and read several more chapters—without needing to snap on the lamp—before dropping back to sleep.

All right, it's not quite *that* bright.

The room might be aglow, but it's still a moon, a component of the night, clandestine and impenetrable.

At one of the high windows of the bedroom, I separate the whimsical white curtains and gaze heavenward, and there it perches—flagrant and almost unholy for all its beaming innocence—staring down on the world. The backyard grass seems jacketed in snow, thick enough for the family of raccoons to leave footprints.

At high-fidelity moments such as this it's not so easy to sift and sort through my feelings. Upon reaching a certain age, one tends to approach new or different sensations skeptically before celebrating or losing heart, searching for rationality and consequences.

But I do know where I am, that much is bit-by-bit apparent by now, and I'm not alone.

No one is.

I'm confident that other individuals also stand at their

windows this very minute, or look on with glazed, sleep-hungry eyes from pre-dawn beds, young or old, it makes no difference, caught up in the tide.

There's no escaping the full moon this night.

And there was no eluding it when, as a boy, I knelt at the window in the little upstairs bedroom on a night of this same tapestry, one of those picture postcard keepsakes, that's what it is—even if it's only the black-and-white flash-back of an alley.

The ribbon of the alley unrolled down to the boulevard two football fields away, and I was the lookout, getting the lay of hobgoblin land.

Halloween it was, the spookiest night of the year, and I had to go out on a witch hunt, dance with ghosts, and all the other characters on the loose.

We've each of us been there and seen the might of the new moon, win or lose, and we're all here tonight, awake or asleep, together, and that's what makes it so grand.

Now is the time to close the bedroom curtains for another night. And I tiptoe to bed without interrupting the soft, comforting breathing of my slumbering wife, and I glide inside the cold sheets.

And wink at the nightlight hanging by the window.

Until we meet again.

Mosquito Gets Oscar

Halloween's dust having settled, and after taking time to ingest its disparities and hilarities, I proclaim that the annual October observation is here to stay.

True, we did hear the customary soap-box sermons denouncing the pagan-rite vestiges of the day and all that. I might disagree with these homilists, but they do make a point. And in this nonpareil land, the "non," the "anti" and the "anti-anti" point-makers do have the freedom to sling their arrows at will.

Regardless, Halloween came, and a multitude of fun people had their flings. Not only kids. There's a party and fancy costume emporium not far from our house, and on the several times I drove by on Halloween weekend, the shop and lot were clogged. In fact, to keep traffic rolling, an officer was called in. Or, possibly, she was only wearing a Keystone Kop costume.

In any case, on a nippy night of a full moon the kids did drop by our place, less scary than cute, to show off their get-ups, to pick up treats, and while they didn't arrive in record numbers, they were mostly from the immediate neighborhood. As it should be. Chaperons, too, were on the lurk, not far behind.

Long ago, the last thing we frolickers of lower grade-school age wanted was our parents tagging along. But that was another age, when the shadows of the street were the exclusive residency of ghosts and hobgoblins.

All of this is not to say that we had nothing to fear out there. Huh, far from it. When certain juveniles felt they were too old to paint their faces with mama's lipstick, or wear false faces and shroud themselves in sheets as we did, they put on Lone Ranger–type masks and roved the streets in search of knavery. Armed to the teeth. With peashooters.

This year, if we'd had an Oscar for top costume, it would've gone to the girl of middle-school age who traversed the gravel of our driveway like a ballerina, and turned out to be a mosquito. That's right, draped in a gossamer-winged, cleverly and intricately designed, hand-sewn original. Colossal. And from out of the dimness on the road came a mother's cue to her daughter to "turn around" for the benefit of the couple standing in the doorway. The voice of the proud designer and seamstress? Take a bow, ma'am.

Yet I was most taken by the night's last callers, a tall, princely boy and three beautiful girls of high-school vintage.

They approached our door in quotidian apparel, but that's irrelevant. I found it refreshingly astonishing that at their ages they could still find enchantment and revelry in this unsophisticated door-to-door ritual. They were polite, open, articulately droll. If they were another faction out to make a point, this one in wholesome behalf of teenagers, they achieved. The treat was ours.

And so another old-fashioned Halloween has come knocking on the door. And gone.

Now, Thanksgiving.

Terry—Friend Indeed

Did you ever wake up in the morning athirst for the sprightliness of bygone days? Surely there have been times when you've thrown back the covers of dawn, and sat on the edge of the bed, and furrowed the webs in your head, and wondered if this might all be just a dress rehearsal. That the next time around life will be easier, that you'll have a starring role in the production, and that the bouquets will be more manifest.

But you know the other side too, walking into the kitchen in the beam of a new day, lighting up a pot of coffee or tea, unfolding the newspaper and spreading out the world on a silver platter before you. And feel the urge to sing a little ditty.

Well, the news isn't always cheery or teeming with promise, but you're at a point when you're starting to put on a few years, and you're still *part* of it, part of everything. That's the glory of it.

And that's the manner of thought one of my friends transmits to me whenever we meet. Although he's half my age, I sometimes think Terry knows twice as much as I do, including, unfortunately, first-hand knowledge of pain. My friend is one of those among us suffering from AIDS. Dying, actually. And about all I can do for him is donate prayers on his behalf.

He never told my wife or me about his disease, not outright, bluffing his way along with robustness and twinkle— though the suspicious signs slowly surfaced. At first when he left his job, we figured he needed more time to shop and do chores for his neighbors and friends.

When my wife and I planned to fly away for a few days, he *informed* us he'd be our chauffeur to the airport.

And later he was parked and waiting in the lane for returning flights.

Terry was a captain in the food services industry, but he also studied medicine in that other life and worked as a nurse, never dreaming he'd be his own patient—so soon.

Several months ago he moved to the west coast of Florida, but was in town recently for all-day tests, and afterward stopped at our place for tea.

How did he feel? Last time we asked that question he said he felt like an eight on a scale of one to ten. This day, he was a four.

Who would guess it? Well, yes, he's shed weight, but you won't find an ounce of self-pity in him. You'd never know that in bed at night his every muscle cries with cramps.

His life has slimmed down to the intensity of simplicity. That's what I love about him, and must remember myself.

He's still a friend indeed for many, his spiritual muscles tuned up. And his communicable grin remains as wide as a hug.

I'm sure he counted his blessings at this year's Thanksgiving Day table, and, knowing Terry, I doubt he demanded a recount.

A Blessing to Count

Life is full of big swindles. This is just the way things happen to be.

As Uncle Lou, who had a way with wayward words, used to put it, you takes the bitter with the sweet—and all that jazzy rhetoric.

Still, fact is, mankind's big deceptions are far outnumbered by the slap-happy hours, and all the simply spectacular chances of life in its plain everyday doses. And that, if we pull up our chairs and think it through, is what Thanksgiving Day adds up to.

On this November morning, I've been sitting here at my desk checking up on myself, fingering along my lifeline that extends back to 1924. Astonishingly, I had to track all the way up to my late teenhood before resurrecting a truly big gyp. Presumably, in the earlier years, I managed to tolerate the usual number of predicaments and frustrations. I say *presumably* because we were one of those classic, forever-strapped-for-cash families. Even so, no incident rated high enough on the chaotic scale to stick with me these many years.

In the big emotional rook alluded to above, of course, I was snatched from civilian life and dressed up in World War II khaki. The thing is, my wish was to stay home and get on with my life in tweeds. Granted, I didn't know yet in which precise direction I wanted to get on, but staying home would've been the better place to work it out.

This is not a woe-is-me song. Plenty guys my age—dolls too—went out the front door, duty-bound, and waved goodbye to their folks, a few of them for the last time.

Even so, those *were* the years classified by experts as prime time. All these years later, however, I'm not so sure about that. I'm thinking that the prime time of my life is *today.*

So all of that aside, I was scooped out of my cozy 1940s mold, but the silver lining is this: I was able to make it home on Thanksgiving Day that year. It was the only blessing I needed to count. Spending the first major holiday without your parents, or without a significant cherished one, can be a heart-twister. Double the lament if you're also bogged in a quagmire.

Well, having finished basic and technical training, I ended up at a pre-debarkation camp fairly near home. That is, within hitchhiking distance of a weekend pass. Although I can't say if Mom fixed a turkey for us, I'm sure we all felt the underlying wartime sadness. My older brother had already sailed off with the navy.

We dined in the kitchen. That's where most of my visit passed. It's where Mom knew contentment. When home, it's where her brood ganged up on her.

No, I never felt deprived because we had no formal dining room.

Actually, in summing up, the biggest gyp I can think of would've been this: if God had sent somebody else to take my place in that family.

You're Welcome

Right around this time of year, seated here at the keyboard, my fingers usually pick out a tune linked to family. Thanksgiving being the season, of course.

This time around, however, my thoughts take a slightly different slant, extending far beyond my own blood lines. Although it's still about family, the human structure I'm talking about today includes you. Welcome to the table.

You're forever welcome, naturally, but I'd like to make sure that newcomers in particular, perhaps someone who hasn't picked up our newspaper or a line of my writing before, is able to find some trustworthy spirit and cordiality.

I'm aware that there's a whole ship of lonesome souls adrift out there for one inescapable reason or another.

Possibly you, yes, you, happen to be reading these words, at this very moment, all by yourself while stuck out at the airport, at the train or bus station, and won't or weren't able to get home for the holiday.

That's tough. I've been there, friend. Who knows if this will help you any, but if nothing else, you and I, in some unfathomable, fantastic way, are presently communicating with one another. Anyone who reads this letter is not alone.

One of the captivating aspects of writing a column is that the author has no way of knowing which—or how many—lucky readers will be perusing the arresting phrases he or she sets forth, or where or whence they'll be ingested. Well, that's elementary to most writing genres, isn't it? Indeed that's the beauty of it. Ah, sweet mystery.

My own preferred place to pore over the daily newspaper is at the breakfast table. Being of sound mind in retirement gives me this leisurely privilege. Consequently it's easy for me to picture readers in similar chairs, even though, truth be known, I don't intentionally consider this angle while fabricating these sentences.

All I know, the process is akin to addressing old friends. Make that *long-time* friends.

Please note, I do take my job seriously. There could be some challenge in this, considering my light-hearted leanings. As a recent example, I observed that the prevailing gloomy outlook in some quarters might be in need of a facelift. And suggested that folks take up the fine art of skipping. I meant it. Yep, literally. So much the merrier if people could whistle at the same time while skipping down the street.

Oh, the timing was ideal for one reader. Her letter fairly gushed with the news that her son had just asked her to teach him how to skip. And that he was also eager to learn to whistle. With tots like him in the wings, I think this old republic is going to be all right.

Ah, Thanksgiving. I could hardly begin my extended thank-you list in this last inch of space. Blessings, all.

Finally, for making my appearance here today possible, I would like to thank my mom and dad.

And readers like you.

Better to Give Than Get

Al's Toggery was the name of the little emporium, located midway in the strip mall three blocks from our house. Nobody called it a strip mall, because that classification had yet to be revealed to an unenlightened shopping public. A strip of a dozen shops, that's it, flanked by a drugstore and by an outdoor vegetable market where fowl and rabbits hung from hooks on cold days.

The area was integral to my life as a juvenile, and although I've not revisited there in fifty years, I can reach into my memory and move the pieces around—as if in a miniature village under a Christmas tree.

And so it was that on a cold mid-December day, I stood with my mom eyeing the wares of the showcase window at Al's Toggery. While the shop featured dry goods, it also displayed an array of toys and games. Mom pointed to a Buck Rogers ray gun and casually asked if I liked it. I shook my head. Aw, what a dreadful blunder. Her face fell under a cloud, and I felt like two-bits. Apparently it'd already been purchased for me for Christmas.

Quick on my feet, I said, "Wait, you mean *this, this* ray gun? Oh, yeah, Mom, it's keen, looks like fun."

Holidays and birthdays would've been much easier for Mom if she'd given birth to three girls instead of three rascals.

Actually, the outlook for games and stuff that year, 1931, looked bleak, judging by Al's wares, most of which would show up under neighborhood Yule trees. Sure, there was also Spot Hardware, a couple of doors down, although the pricey kid stuff handled by those folks—bicycles, BB guns, baseball mitts, and such—were beyond the fantasies of the average rascal. But it was a splendid place for browsing. Long and narrow, bloated with items that broke the barrier of my imagination, the store smelled of friction tape and hammers and linseed oil. For a long time I associated that essence with Christmas.

We, the young, I reckon, could've been accused of obsession in regards to the gifts Santa or his agent had in store for us—what we were going to *get* on Christmas morn.

And yet, was it so punishable?

I don't think so. We were good little boys and girls, were we not? Thanks to our parents, teachers and preachers, we knew the inside story of the first Christmas, set in a stable in Bethlehem two thousand years ago.

Still, no denying, there was something magnetic about the worldly side of the picture, too.

As the big day drew nearer, our house filled with secrets. People bustled in and out. Mom's oven shifted into high gear.

We were building our memories, our future lifeline.

As we matured—or so we were told—we'd also learn that giving, rather than receiving, is the far, far better thing. But just how old does a person have to be to get the hang of that?

Here I sit, still excitedly wondering what I'll get this Christmas.

Stringing Us Along

Nosing around under the temporary tree in our living room a few days before Christmas, I detected no small, cube-shaped present with my name attached.

Seemingly this meant, and as it did indeed turn out, no one had purchased a yo-yo for me as a gift.

Not that I nursed any unspoken hankering for one of those little spools on a string, but recently my spouse did call my attention to the report that the sale of yo-yos had reached an all-time high. You could've fooled me. True, I don't hang around playgrounds and school bus stops, but I've witnessed no evidence of a yo-yo craze in or around my urban cranny.

At any rate, when my wife asked if I'd owned a yo-yo during my boyhood, I mistakenly speculated that just for nostalgic kicks she'd surprise me with one on Christmas morn.

Actually, just about every boy in the 1930s had one in his pocket. Or, in the case of big families, there was at least one in every household. Some girls held their own in this field, but mostly it was a male thing, like playing leapfrog.

The inmates of my grammar school were introduced to the fine art of yo-yoing by a young, wiry fellow from, appropriately, the Philippines. Centuries before, as legend avers, Filipinos developed the yo-yo as a weapon in the hunting of small prey and for ambushing enemies while hiding in trees. Lawdy, the splendors that the young fellow could perform with that doohickey—"walk the dog" and "rock the cradle" and "around the world" and more— while we school children gathered round him in awe.

As intended, this demonstration precipitated a land-office blitz in the purchase of yo-yos at our neighborhood confectioneries and variety stores. The things couldn't have cost more than a nickel or a dime apiece, and yet that turned out to be a big gyp. See, if you wanted to dazzle the girls or your grandma by performing *all* the tricks, you needed the bigger, glossy, deluxe model—called a "sleeper," I think. Probably set you back two-bits easy.

On our troop ship out of New Guinea, bound for the Philippines in early 1945, I half expected that we'd be hooking up with a crack, deadly company of native yo-yoists, wiry young fellows who could wipe out an enemy detail without the firing of one shot.

Alas, another major disappointment.

During and after the war over there I didn't even see a *child* spinning or carrying a yo-yo. There's a theory that the Japanese military, while still having its own way in that country, confiscated all the yo-yos and shipped 'em back home.

Well, there were any number of curious theories and schemes emanating from Tokyo and Washington—in those days. Still are.

All I can tell you for sure, folks, beware the New Year, because there are a lot of yo-yos roaming around out there in our world.

Long Night's Bus Ride

It was just one of those things, one of those contemptible things you can't do anything about. I overslept.

How incredibly dumb. But it was done. I missed the train.

I'd worked late at the newspaper office, walked half a mile to my bachelor's cottage, packed an overnight bag, then flopped across the bed to rest my eyes, as the saying goes. Next thing I knew, it was after midnight.

Groggily I dialed the depot with an outside hope that the train might be late. No such luck. It'd come and gone, well on its way clickety-clacking toward St. Louis and points north.

Quickly I rang the bus station. Yes, there'd be a bus in an hour. Scooping up my bag, I dog-trotted all the way to the station. As it turned out, the bus was running an hour late. Just one of those nights. Finally the bus did come rolling in, whisking the sleepyhead off to Christmas Day with his mom. Whisking? Unfortunately it was not an express bus. The driver pulled off into every burg he could find, and some, I swear, that he searched for and ultimately gave up on.

What I remember most about that Christmas Eve is the hiss of air brakes all through the night. And the smell was all wrong—sweaty socks, soiled diapers, cigarette butts, abandoned sandwiches.

Where was the scent of homemade cookies and holiday bread, the essence of citron, anise, walnuts, chocolates? Also recalled was the fragrance of sprigs from Christmas trees past that my dad would let smolder on the lids of the potbelly stoves. One step inside that house, and you knew exactly the season 'twas.

There'd be no more of that. The potbellies were long gone, and my dad had died seven months before. This was Mom's first Christmas without him in nearly forty years. And the lonesomeness in her voice was clear when I called from a rest stop, hours after I should've been there.

"Where *are* you?" she said.

I felt like a cad, explaining what'd happened. But before she'd know it, I'd be pulling up in front of her place in a taxi like a big shot and kissing the top of her head.

She laughed, and it was the best Christmas gift she could've given me, better than the smell of home. At least she knew where I was. That's important to mothers.

Reboarding the bus, I told the driver I had a hot date to keep, and would he please "step on the gas?"

He laughed. Two laughs in a row. Not bad. I think he needed that laugh as much as I. It couldn't have been much fun for him, hauling us over the hills and through the hamlets. On that night of nights. Unless he, too, was hastening home.

I closed my eyes, and presently dozed off, listening to the hymn of air brakes.

My dad, wearing a bus driver's cap, shook me awake, welcoming his little boy to another bright Christmas morn.

Early One Christmas Morn

My pal Raymond and I were chosen ones:
hand-picked to serve as acolytes on Christmas morn.

The only hitch, the scene of honor was not our parish church a few short blocks away—rather an orphanage chapel, a forty-five-minute hike into the face of icy gusts. And we'd have to check in by 5:30 A.M.

None of this struck my dad as tidings of a particularly rousing, holiday nature. Despite my reminders that I was thirteen and capable of setting an alarm clock myself, Dad and I both knew he'd be up first that morning, making sure the kitchen was warm for the honoree as he dressed by the potbelly stove.

Not unexpectedly, my mom came shivering into the kitchen, and before I—sweatered and jacketed—could get out the door she lassoed me with a long red neck scarf and lashed it over my ears. I felt like an Egyptian mummy. She gave me a God's-speed kiss, and sent me into one of the coldest, most elegant nights of my life.

Ours was a lower middle class neighborhood, but on this Christmas pre-dawn, under deep chaste snow and a searchlight moon, I could've been tramping anywhere in the world. The air pinched my nostrils. Lamplights were the only figures I passed along the way to Raymond's home. And not a lick of illumination shimmered inside his two-story domicile.

Now what? Knock on the door, terrify the whole household?

Secretly I hoped he'd overslept, leaving me to continue on my bittersweet trek alone, heroically, led by the star, warmed by my mission and by visions of my parents back in bed, and by my two brothers in the attic, slumbering peacefully in featherbed heaven.

All at once the storm door at Raymond's place cracked open. Ice fell from its hinges like breaking glass. But not a light woke up in the house behind my partner as he silently descended the satiny stone steps. The night was big enough and cold enough for two martyrs.

Fearful of inciting neighborhood dogs, we spoke in frosty whispers while plowing ahead, then not at all, the cold having distorted our lips. I yearned for the animal warmth of a stable.

It turned out to be a private Mass for the nuns of the orphanage, a privilege for any individual of any faith to attend, a service of sedate sublimity, sullied only by the random growls of Raymond's stomach. Before we headed back out into the beastly, waiting wind, the mother superior, in devout silence, presented each altar boy with a beribboned Baby Ruth candy bar.

The sun was up by the time I arrived home and opened the kitchen door to a sumptuous burst of warmth. The rest of the family had been to church, and my dad was fixing breakfast.

I don't remember any presents exchanged on that 1937 Christmas, except one, and I took it from my jacket, and I gave it to my mom—a frozen Baby Ruth.

The Newest Star

You don't have to believe this story. I heard it the first time from my dad long ago.

It's a magnetic story, and seasonal, although, admittedly, it commands a degree of tolerance and sensitivity on the part of listener or reader. In any event, the story began more than two thousand years ago, and shows little sign of diminishing.

It's the tale of a baby boy, born in what we in this nation cite as a foreign land—and under less than jolly conditions. Oh, but the lights on all the porches of heaven came on that night, and every angel gathered around to sing in awesome harmony to celebrate the event.

Below, quietly, the scene was a cave, a stable, the only overnight accommodations the travelers, a couple, could find. After the mother delivered the babe herself, a few simple shepherds, guided by a bright new star, came round to pay their respects.

This same star attracted three wise men who revered the babe as they might a king, presenting expensive gifts—most of them left behind for the poor.

Next night, the father of the new family was nudged awake by an angel and exhorted to take his wife and baby and flee this city threatened by deadly political intrigue and moral disorder.

The ensuing years passed pleasantly as the boy studied religiously, obeyed his parents—a point my dad underscored—and learned carpentry, the trade of his father.

At age thirty, he left home. A mild man, he slid into his sandals and roamed the countryside preaching peace and goodwill to all, the doctrine of loving one's neighbor, and that it's better to give than to receive.

"See, there was a lot of funny stuff going on in the world back then, too," as my dad put it, "and he told everybody to behave themselves."

During his three-year crusade the man cultivated quite a following, and his reputation spread. His popularity, in fact, did him in, breeding jealousy, contempt, slander, deceit, and, most woefully, a plot for murder.

But his message remains crisp today, and I think that's the part that so impressed my dad, another mild-mannered man. That the hero of our story, born in a stable, who had the audacity to announce that he was out to save the world, still inspires such allegiance.

The history of mankind is divided into two volumes: before his birth, and after. That's no fairy tale.

Historians accept December twenty-fifth as his birthday. This same month we have the feast day of Nicholas, the gift-giving, fourth-century saint. Ah, soon enough the legends emerged: Jolly St. Nick, Kris Kringle, Father Christmas, Santa Claus. The season, called Christmas, also became a commercial windfall, but there are worse sins. It's still colored with giving, with rewards for the well-behaved, still a time for sugar and spicy sausages and all things nice, faith and miracles.

Another Christmas has come. Step outside tonight. Look around. The lights of hope still burn.

We Do! We Do!

Getting Our Kicks in Pottstown

Our twentieth wedding anniversary weekend did not get off to a flying start. We tumbled from bed before dawn Friday, to check in at Orlando International two hours before the 8:05 takeoff.

So much for optimism. We shuffled aboard at 9:05. The airline had to shuttle a "rested" crew in to run the aircraft. Which, all in all, sounded like a sensible idea.

At last everybody settled in, buckled up, and the jet rolled back a few feet onto the tarmac. And there we sat for the next hour and forty minutes.

Evidently the computer had hit the skids. In lay language, our magnificent flying machine lacked sufficient thrust to get off the ground.

The well-rested captain kept passengers informed regarding attempts to reboot the computer, saying they had the manual out and all that stuff. Very heartening.

Finally, in the air, the crew thanked us for our patience with soft drinks and petite bags of pretzels.

But all travails were forgotten when my wife's daughter, wearing a smile bigger than a family-sized pizza, spread welcoming arms to her mom in the Philadelphia airport. She lives an hour's drive away, with her generous husband, daughter, and son, in an idyllic Pottstown subdivision cut into the middle of a forest.

Most important, we'd arrived in time to watch grand-daughter Lauren, then nine, compete in her soccer tournament Saturday morning.

On the eve of her big show she magnanimously yielded her doll-like trundle bed upstairs to us Florida visitors—and bedded down cozily on a spacious living room sofa.

Later, when I sat on the detached trundle to undo my shoes, it tilted and I ended up on the floor with bedding atop me.

Early Saturday, after a feast of flapjacks, we were at the athletic spread, and there I was, roaming the sidelines with a camera, gleefully flashing back to my days as a one-man sports department—my first newspaper job—forty-seven years ago. I'd hoped to snap a pic of Lauren kicking the winning goal, but she *was* on field when it happened. Her Eagles finished the season undefeated. Hip-hip. Fitting reward for her coach, for he's a jolly good fellow, a dedicated sort who sent no boy or girl on or off the field without commendation.

I eavesdropped on a woman coach giving her players a halftime pep talk. At the conclusion a little girl looked up at her and said, "I like your nails."

Naturally there was more to our weekend, and we wouldn't have missed it for all the tea in Beijing. True, my wife and I'd considered revisiting friends and sites in Ireland and England to ritualize our twentieth anniversary, but how could we not accept Lauren's invitation? What're relatives for? Phone and e-mail dialogues are grand, but every so often it seems important to touch, look at one another, talk and laugh together, and, yes, maybe cry a little, eye to eye.

Anyway, as they say on postcards, had a great time, weather beautiful, wish you'd been there.

Come, Get Old with Me

Today being your birthday, my dear and faithful wife, I'd planned to pen words soft and sentimental, maybe even mushy.

Something, however, happened on the way to the keyboard. I kept getting rudely nudged in the ribs—by the uncompromising reality of this year's bumper crop of crushing, abhorrent newspaper and television headlines. Thus, it seemed clearly appropriate that I should step up today and say something on the subject because, alas, the natives, more so than ever, appear to be getting restless, and unhealthily fearful.

I'd say that both fundamentally and alarmingly, the brooding and stewing of the rank-and-file is focused on the worldly madness that's being bequeathed to their children, their grandchildren. A commendable anxiety, indubitably.

But hold the phone, folks. Are they forgetting their history lessons? Haven't we faced and outlasted Depression, World War II, and other confrontations, including terrorism, vandalism, discrimination, and drought?

Just when the masses think they've seen everything in this world—they probably have. As the Bible notes, there are no new wrinkles under the sun. Or under a new moon, come to that.

I don't even think of my freshly discovered facial wrinkles—which you, my dear, have discreetly unmentioned— as new. Worry and laugh lines of character simply take decades—seven in my particular case—to surface. It's doubtful that many folks are going around wearing wrinkle implants.

One day this week, as you prepared an evening meal, a voice on the kitchen radio informed you that the vaunted internet highway of communication could be brought right into our home. Irked, you swirled and glared at the radio and said, "I don't *want* the internet highway in my home!" Remember?

Later, you made light of your little outburst: "That's probably the way some people first felt about the telephone."

Exactly. That's what I'm talking about. We've been through it all before, in one way or another, either in the name of progress or retrogression. Watching the nightly news, it's easy to forget that the good guys still outnumber the bad. That's the good news.

People still have unfailing faith. They do more than just hang in there. They get up early, work hard, study, teach, make merry, marry, raise children, build their castles, and *celebrate* anniversaries and birthdays.

Birthdays? Does that sound like a cue, my dear, that I'm about to reveal how many years ago this date you were born? Fret not, my lady. You know your lover better than that. Nobody'd believe how old you are anyway.

So, all that having been duly recorded, readers shouldn't go away with the sense that I'm impassive about our jittery world. There's much that settles heavily upon me. Oh, yes. I, too, sporadically feel the swarming unfairness of it all.

As an example, why is it taking so long for the character lines to surface on *your* face, sweetheart? I keep telling you to hurry up and get old with me, but you won't listen.

Regardless, happy birthday, luv.

Happy Mum's Day

"I wish," she said, *"I still looked the way I* did when we met, when you fell in love with me."

What could I say? "You do, you *do!*" No, my wife hates lying worse than mushy tomatoes. Even little white lies nettle her. Or, in my case, little gray ones. Believe me, it's not easy being married to an honest woman.

Truth is, my wife does look older than she did on the historic day when she tried to pick me up downtown. There I was innocently talking to a friend on the corner, and there she came sashaying up the sidewalk. No, she didn't drop her handkerchief while passing by.

She stopped. Approached. Spoke.

In a way I wish she had allowed her hanky to flutter to the walk. I used to watch women employ that come-hither ploy in the old movies, and wished it'd happen to me one day. Never did. And I've about given up hope it might. To be honest, I dropped my own handkerchief a time or two over the years, but that didn't work either. Those handkerchiefs are probably still blowing around out there in the winds of time.

Dreams aside, here's what occurred on the street corner. She recognized me from the mugshot the newspaper ran with my daily masterpieces, and complimented me.

Did I ask her name, get her telephone number as Clark Gable or Cary Grant surely would've? Foolishly, I didn't. But the fates were on our side. Some months later we met again—in a hotel room.

She was there for a presentation at a teachers' convention, and I as a journalist, a member of the working press who, ladies and gentlemen, was about to fall in love.

After her songs and stories, we talked at length.

Leaving, I said. "I'll see you in my dreams." So help me. Schmaltzy, admittedly, but it worked.

Incidentally, when I say my wife looks older than she did back then, this doesn't imply she looks *old*. Certainly not as outmoded as I, but then I had a running headstart on her in this world.

Don't know if I'll still be around when she does turn old. If ever. Ageless is a word that fits easily on individuals who get excited by great music and literature, and passing butterflies.

Anyway, she's the one who brought up the subject. Women are known to do this when they look into the mirror of a calendar and suddenly realize they must face up to another birthday.

Hers, as I pen these words, falls on Wednesday of next week. I'm not telling her age. But Sunday is her twenty-ninth Mother's Day, believe it or not.

Happy birthday, luv.

And to you and to mums everywhere: Happy Mother's Day every day!

A few weeks back as she sat smiling at a 1950s photo of me, my wife said. "I wish I'd known you back then."

She thought that over. "Well, I don't know, maybe I wouldn't have liked you."

Exactly. I say it's worked out just fine.

Let's Catch a Train

Most folks in my circle haven't ridden a railroad train in years. Some, sadly, have never been inside a boxcar, caboose, coach, or compartment.

Compartment. Now *there's* an exciting word to unpack from one's bag of recollections. For me as a young fellow steeped in mystery novels and talking pictures, the word betokened class, luxury, and, yes, intrigue.

What could be grander, I thought, than to book a private room on the 20th Century Limited, Grand Central Station to Chicago, then on to Los Angeles aboard the storied Super Chief?

In a later year I did blow my entire piggybank on a roomette, St. Louis to L.A., but it was a cramped facsimile of a compartment, and not as compelling as anticipated. Intrigue failed to drop in for a visit.

My wife and I hadn't been on a train in thirty years, and never together, and so on a whim we made reservations. We'd depart Amtrak's station in Orlando at 1:38 P.M., arriving in Tampa at 3:22. After a bit of browsing, and maybe an early-bird dinner, we'd leave Tampa at 6:22, arriving back in our town at 8:38. An excursion, a simple adventure, see if we could shake loose some spirits from the old days in a few hours.

It was during World War II, of course, and shortly afterward, that railroad passenger service in this country hit its summit. Lord, what a beehive our Union Station in St. Louis was. It's a shopping mall today, but back then trains arrived and departed on a dozen or more tracks, loudspeaker messages filled the air, and the bootblacks never stopped snapping their cloths.

My wife, when a child, was enchanted by train breakfasts and those ice water cabinets and paper cups in each car.

Once I stood in awe in an open vestibule of a troop train on a subzero midnight, hemmed in by the walls of Colorado, and the next day we threw up the windows to catch sight and scent of orange groves. Magnifico.

So, finally, the day of our trip.

My wife packed a book, a notebook, and a Granola bar for each of us, but before going out I'd call Amtrak, check if the train was on schedule.

"Good thing you called, sir," said a woman from a remote switchboard. "The Orlando train is two hours and twenty-four minutes late out of Savannah. He might make up a few minutes . . ."

And then maybe he wouldn't. Or it could even be later. We could visualize ourselves disembarking in Tampa and sprinting to catch the 6:22 train back home. If lucky.

Reluctantly, the reservations were cancelled.

Because we were dressed for the road we piled in our automobile and headed for New Smyrna Beach. The ocean, beach, and fresh breeze were inspiriting, and at four o'clock we motored over to the mainland for a leisurely fish dinner. All in all a pleasant outing. That's normally the way our times together turn out, but we did admit to a letdown that our train trip back to yesterday didn't pan out.

Maybe another day.

Dreaming on Featherbeds

"Oh, look, here's an ad for a featherbed."

"A real featherbed? Let me see that," said I, rinsing the drippings of peaches and strawberries from my fingers, then with towel in hand joining my wife in the dining area. She showed me the illustrated advertisement in the morning newspaper.

"You're right, that's what it says, but who're they trying to josh? It looks like a mattress, if you ask me."

I explained that a featherbed was nothing more than a big bag made out of mattress ticking, stuffed with feathers, and used as an additional *cover* to snuggle oneself into bed on blustery nights. Leastwise, that was my maternal Grandma's rendition of the product, and that dear person's briefings and traditions—and superstitions too—have carried me a long way in this world.

"What kind of feathers?" my mate wanted to know.

"Well, I don't know," said I, circling back to my breakfast chores in the kitchen, "chicken feathers, I guess, turkey, and goose feathers. Grandma kept chickens year round."

When it came time for one of her hens to enact the supreme sacrifice, Grandma would traipse out to the coop, select the right bird, and unceremoniously wring its neck. It baffled me how this woman, my mom's mom, the sweetest individual—and the leading cook and baker—on the block, could perpetrate this stunt so imperturbably.

Afterward, whenever I'd overhear the exasperated homemaker next door snap at her husband, "Sox, I could wring your neck," the phrase didn't sound so funny anymore.

Today, looking back, my guess is that we—that'd include my two brothers and our two male cousins from the neighborhood—all were privileged to spend snuggly nights under Grandma's featherbed in the big upstairs bed in her old frame house. Possibly all on the same shivery night—once or twice.

I do know we all spent a rollicking hour or so together in Grandma's bathtub on at least one summer day. Wait, it's possible my older brother decided to forgo this gala event, figuring himself too old for juvenile antics and cutting up. But let me say this for the old boy. His attitude along these lines has improved with age.

You know, there's something cozily exquisite and safe just talking about featherbeds, and about this business of being tucked into bed at night. I'd speculate that most of us savored the tuck-in experience as children, and again when putting our own youngsters to bed. The night was nervous until the whole brood was safely home and under cover. Ah, that's the ticket, especially nowadays with the world off on a jittery spin.

Yesterday, when my spouse and I were ready to call it a day, we were rather reluctant to let it go. It'd been time well spent, and love was on our side. And yet, once we slid safely between the sheets, we both said *ahhh*. I think that's what it all amounts to.

No, we didn't need a featherbed, but it was definitely that kind of feeling.

You May Skip This

I awoke, arose from the bed, appropriated my wife's hand, and away we went, skipping merrily through the house.

You like that picture?

Well, sorry, we didn't do that at all. However, I did give the gleeful, freewheeling act a moment's affirming thought—not that I believed for a minute I could truly pull it off.

Now, four days later, I'm unable to come up with a fitting explanation as to what urged my mind to jog along those lines. Not that it matters terribly. It's a blessing to wake up with a gush in the old veins—regardless of how misleading or fleeting.

I actually did ask my wife if she cared to accompany me on a hand-in-hand caprice through our little cottage. She chortled. It was too early for an out-and-out laugh.

Had she said yes, *then* you might've heard full-bodied laughter—mine.

About this matter of *skipping*. I'm not so sure I ever performed that particular act—hopping lightly ahead on alternating feet—in my whole life. At the back of my mind I have the word catalogued as a girl thing to do. Like skipping rope.

Although I wasn't so lucky as to have sisters, there was plenty of rope skipping—or jumping rope, as it might've been called in your neighborhood—to observe on our block or up in the school playground.

In some quarters this game might've been judged a sissified undertaking for boys, and yet there's reasonable doubt in my mind that many of us ordinary fellows had the agility and grace to match the girls at it. Or look as good in the doing.

Ah, and how exciting it was, spying on the little misses in their middy blouses and pleated skirts doing the advanced, Double Dutch, *two*-rope version of this recreation.

It's been so long ago that I can't remember when last I viewed any young people jumping or skipping rope. Where'd they all go?

And at one time it seemed fairly common to see a boy just plain skipping happily down the alley, or a pair of girls, hand in hand, skipping along the sidewalk. Where'd they all skip off to? It's a mislaid art, that's what it is, like whistling a merry tune.

Have the kids out there lost the beat for freedom, nonchalance, and rash abandonment?

And how about the more mature populace? No kidding. Well, it's rather unlikely that the older skippers will soon be replacing our army of grim joggers all over the place. In a way that's a pity. I'm thinking our country could use a facelift. So many people on the TV news and in the papers—except for election winners—look so dismal, so desperate.

Granted, skipping isn't as easy as it looks. You have to be long on stamina, short on self-consciousness.

And if you want to really be successful at it while skipping down your street, and make a difference in the world, see if you can whistle at the same time.

Good to the Last Morsel

My wife never needs to inquire as to which serving of her main course I liked best. All she has to do is wait to see which tidbit ends up as the last bite on my fork. The old save-the-best-for-last game.

Sunday morning's choice, however, proves somewhat trickier. That's when the game usually boils down to the last morsels of low-fat bacon and sausage, and the yellow remnant of one coddled egg. Actually, it's not unheard of for all three to wind up together on the final stab of my fork.

On the other hand, my wife herself isn't quite as predictable an eater as I, although there was a time, during her girlhood, when one edible in particular, whenever served, *always* remained on her plate till last. And no matter how assiduously she prayed, or sobbingly beseeched her papa to take it away, the dreaded slice of fried liver just wouldn't vanish. To this very day she hates liver as much—well, as much as I lap it up.

Long before I met my wife—this would be in my twenties—I dated a knockout redhead. I never got around to finding out how she felt about liver and onions, but she *did* preach a doctrine converse to the game plan of save-best-for-last. Example—eating the crust first on a slice of her favorite pie—a procedure she once faithfully practiced—didn't make sense to her.

"I learned that by the time I'd come to the saved part,"she said, "I was too full to enjoy it."

Ergo, she evolved as a grabby individual in general. Or so it seemed. In short order I stopped seeing her. That was fifty-five years ago, and I still don't miss her.

But you know, over the years, I've sporadically pondered the connection between humans and their gastronomic habits. You've heard the saying, "We are what we eat." So how about serial killers, bushwhackers, charlatans, rapists, swindlers, con men, and con women, do they relish the same kinds of food I do?

Last Sunday a young Australian friend of mine, chatting with his parents back home via telephone, learned that his mother had been the victim of road rage. What caused that enraged perpetrator—or any copy-cat perp here or down under—to blow his top? He followed my friend's mother home, weaving maniacally in traffic, and vowed to return to get her.

Was it something he ate that morning? Did his attitude, perhaps, have anything to do with table manners? Don't smirk. Had no parent at the family table ever educated him in the importance of being patient, polite, temperate? Tipped him off about the last being first?

Oh. Before I take my leave here, in case it's not clear, my wife is a crackerjack cook. *Anything* she prepares will stand up as a last morsel on *my* plate.

OK, unless it's a Brussels sprout.

Speaker of the House

I switch on the air-cooling unit in my study. That's all I hear now, the low hum, and the clack of keys of my magnificent writing machine.

This is one of the advantages of being a retired stiff—as opposed to a *working* stiff.

Oh, yes, a few times, while still salaried, I longed to slip into seclusion this way, wave away the crash and clatter of telephones, typewriters, news-spewing contraptions, and wisecracks.

I suppose we all had—and some still have—abrasive distractions at our locations of labor, but we work around them, and, in time, become accustomed to the vibrations, as we do to the sounds of our homes.

A home has its own characteristic sounds, unique as its scents and secrets. Have you ever awakened abruptly in the night wondering where you are? It's a moment of near panic, but I have only to lie in bed and listen, and catch the steady, soothing swing of the clock pendulum in my study, and know I'm home.

During my childhood it was a big windup alarm clock ticking away in the kitchen or on the floor beside my dad's bed. On wintry nights you could hear the bones of our old house—already ancient the day we moved in—snap and crackle. Dad calmed our fears. The old gal was just settling in for the night.

When my wife and I switch off our bedside reading lights, the lampshades transmit eccentric, sporadic pops, muted signals that somehow compliment the house's rhythm. My mate gives me a quizzical look. Yes, we'll have to look into this phenomenon, but the lamps, I know, are only settling in for the night.

Birds babbling, the nocturnal fleeting steps of raccoons on the roof, and on summer nights frogs blowing their toy horns in recital down by the lake, everything is part of the house's history.

But one of the most hopeful of external noises: the United Parcel Service truck. We don't get much traffic on our dead-end road, so the two girls who once lived here learned early to identify the arrival of the truck in the neighborhood. And they'd dart expectantly to the front of the house. Too often, UPS with its truckload of goodies passed them by. Over recent holidays the truck made almost daily stops at our doorstep. Lamentably, the girls no longer live here.

Suddenly, now, blue of mood, I strain for sounds outside my four walls. No, I don't miss the workplace, but I do listen for evidence that my wife, overdue from a junket, has returned. I arise. I saunter. The rooms stand empty. But the house continues to breathe, is never mute, not even when the fridge motor takes a break and drops its bomb of familiar silence.

What endowments have I made to the stored sounds of this house? Am I responsible for the tears or the laughter?

Then at last there it is, wheels crunching into the gravel of our driveway. My wife is home. The impeccable sound.

It's Hard to Say About Pies

My wife said, "If I were to bake a pie this morning, what kind would you like?"

"Gee," I said, "that's hard to say."

"No, it's not hard at all," she said, "just say it."

This little give-and-take is one of the word amusements we sporadically dabble in, but when we converse in regards to selecting my favorite pie, it truly is hard to say. She has quite the proven repertoire for me to choose from.

At any rate, my wife knows how to start off my day with a shebang. You see, pie also happens to be one of my favorite *words,* ranking high on the chart with love, gentle, spring, supper, funny, rosy, girl, book, and nap.

"Pecan?" she said. "How about a nice pecan pie?"

"I wouldn't say no," said I.

Maybe it's only my imagination, but there seems to be something awfully nice, something definitely warm and chummy in the air—above and beyond aroma—when the subject of pies is brought up.

Here's an idea worth exploring. Next time those two opposing mediators sit down at the table of unification in Northern Ireland, they should make provision for a pie break—shamelessly aimed at turning the hardest of hearts to marshmallow.

It'd work like this. At the designated hour, Catholic and Protestant housewives would circulate among the delegates, serving a piece of freshly baked homemade pie to each, along with a cup of coffee or tea.

"Well," said my wife, "let's see, are you in the mood for a nice lemon meringue pie?"

"Always in the mood," said I. Long before I learned to spell it, lemon meringue had been sitting atop my preference list.

Also, I remember—too vividly, really—the women of our church asking my mom to bring a pie to their autumn covered-dish supper. This was in the early 1960s, she was a widow and living with me, and crippling arthritis was slowly crushing her to death. I should've put my foot down, asked the good women to excuse her, but she felt obligated and agreed to bring a pie.

That night at the long banquet table, one of the sponsoring women took one bite of Mom's lemon meringue and shoved it aside, grumbling, "Made with a mix." I don't think Mom, across the table, heard her, thank goodness. If she did, we never discussed it.

My heart held no enmity for the other woman. She didn't realize it was my mom's pie, nor was she cognizant that she was sitting across from the person who once reigned as the best maker of pie crusts in the Western World.

And what *I* wasn't aware of: it'd be the last pie Mom would ever make.

It's hard to say what there is about pies, but incontrovertibly they do bring out the best in certain people—like the golden-brown, fragrant pecan pie my wife slid from her steadfast conventional oven today.

"Walnut, actually,"she said. "I ran out of pecans."

A Piece of Cake

After a long and rainy weekend up north, my wife was due back in Orlando on a late Sunday night flight. Good timing. Monday was her birthday.

Some folks spin into intractable hysteria when stung with reminders that their spouses' birthdays are but a few days hence.

That doesn't happen in our domicile. Whenever confounded for gift ideas, we know that a book or two will bail us out.

As it so happened this year, I bought her three volumes: poetry, fiction, biography.

By their shapes she always knows what is sealed inside my highly lacking wrapping, and that's all right, but if she plays the usual game, she'll pick up the present, shake it this way and that, all the while pretending to guess its contents.

Next I stopped at the nearby deli for a cut of smoked white fish. My wife considers this a decided treat when served on a lightly buttered onion bagel, particularly at breakfast on days designed for celebration. In my late years I've become a shameless rah-rah fan of this combo myself.

Then I rang up one of my favorite above-average restaurants to make a Monday luncheon reservation for two.

Sunday, I did think about chasing the vacuum cleaner around the house as another surprise for my missus, but since it was a day of rest I compromised, turning out a load of laundry—after church—and tucking up the bed with fresh linen.

Ultimately, our Monday together ripened handsomely, as planned, with a few small unforeseen delights tossed in.

Then the sword fell.

Near twilight, in the kitchen, she finally had to say it. "Forgive me for asking, and don't be upset," she said, "but did you forget, or did you not want me to have it because I'm getting fat?"

My heart hit the floor in a splat. Would you believe I'd forgotten to make arrangements for a *birthday cake*?

How *could* I? I wanted to cry, and maybe I did, a drop. Oh, how much better it would've been had the books or the white fish and bagels or *any* of the above and all together been overlooked.

One must understand that the unconditionally sweet birthday cake, ordered from a specialty bakery, had been a tradition in this house for my wife and her two daughters for more than three decades. And if any portion of the cake remained after the party, it was always stored in the freezer where, over the ensuing days, the resident women could steal the occasional gnaw.

Several years ago when the owner of the storied restaurant/bakery unforgivably closed for good, we began purchasing our cakes at the supermarket.

"Don't move," I told my wife, sprinting for the door. "Be right back."

But she hopped in the car with me and we sped to the market and procured a cake with her name hastily inscribed thereon.

Back home, in the twilight in the kitchen, I lit a single candle, and sang dramatically to the happy, happy birthday girl.

It's About Time

Nine o'clock is probably my favorite stop on the clock.

I reach that deduction after cool deliberation, using the generous, happy face of the pendulum clock on the wall of my study as the stage of my musing. I settled on 9 o'clock, not because it's just another pretty face. A mere glimpse of the number sends my mind racing backwards in time, the way memory does, fingering through dusty calendars for some precise, charmed event.

All right, here it is, my first black-and-white recollection of 9. When the clock struck that hour on evenings of the great grammar-school years, Mom and Dad expected their three sons to be inside the house—and the door locked.

Yes, a curfew of sorts—but not quite so unsparing as that. It meant the day was done and we were all tucked in, willingly, safely, snugly, together.

Now was the time for the town crier walking the gas-lit street to bellow, "Nine o'clock and all is well!" And it really *was*.

Town criers prevailed before my time, actually, but I do remember the moody gaslights that kept the streets lonely and safe at night.

Nine o'clock also struck in the morning, though not with the same serendipity, especially on those glowering Mondays. Even so it was a milestone time, the world throwing open the doors again, tumbling the children out of their homes, shouting goodbyes to moms and dads, the even mix of boys and girls congregating in the school house, packing their fears and smiles and smells, time to learn, time to *be* somebody.

We Do! We Do!   151

And isn't it a pity we didn't know what we were about at the time?

And then 5 o'clock.

Ah, not so easy for a daydreamer to forget either, the bittersweet hour, the signal to drag oneself away from the games, wash hands and faces, comb hair, set the kitchen table. Dad would soon be home from his job downtown and we'd all be gathering around for the punctual 5:30 ritual, a banquet every night.

In time, in the dance of the digits, I got to know 5 o'clock in the *morning* quite well too, even though it wouldn't steal meaningfully into my life for a few years yet—during my journalism days, with a world war wedged between.

Seven o'clock appears on my nocturnal clock with a whimsical flourish of its mermaid's tail. And up at the old neighborhood picture show it's time for the auditorium to darken and the screen blaze and the music commence—my first encounter with enchantment.

I sit now at my desk in my study, and hear it plainly tick-tock, tock-tick, the steady beat, and where it stops nobody knows.

On the wall, back over my left shoulder, the timeless numbers stand patient watch, waiting their turns, slim and plump and true. Oh, the stories they could spin.

The story of the moment is that my wife will soon be calling me in to dinner for two.

All is well.

I Do, I Do!

With very little aforethought, we simply went ahead and took the big step.

And so there we were in the earlier part of a warm June morn, the woman and I, standing stalwartly in the chapel, ready to proclaim the old familiar words to one another.

There'd been no time to assemble a supporting cast, although it's hardly likely we would've done so regardless. Essentially the service was a private matter, including the gracious, vested pastor who'd overnight found a space on his overcrowded calendar to oblige us. Afterward we could discuss the event with others, celebrate it, share our feelings with family and friends, stranger or acquaintance, anyone who happened to touch our day.

Majestically, then, without music or flowers, the ceremonial commenced.

I, by tradition, spoke first. And wondered: Is this the way the nuptial dialogue will always be, the man awarded the opening lines? No, probably not, not in a rapidly shifting world that seems preoccupied with frisking and altering all the conventions and mores, for better or for worse.

Be that as it may or may not be, this is the way it was on a day most recent when the world, just for a little while, stood still for a man and a woman with love in mind.

But honesty is called for here. Although I did *so* want to remember each spoken word—as prompted by the presiding man of the cloth—I now find myself unable to write them down precisely. Perhaps because they're jumbled up with all the versions of recitations I've overheard in churches and synagogues and theaters over the years, or read in books.

No matter. One statement at least has stuck to the ribs

of my memory, the part where I vowed to be faithful to my woman. That covers a multitude of lapses.

My wife revealed later that as she listened to my promises, she'd silently responded in her heart, "I know, I *know*." Admitting she found my pledges easier to believe than when first I uttered them by rote, in a similar setting, years ago.

And so I slipped the rings back on her fingers in this celebration of renewing our marital vows, and we joined our hands with priestly hands, to tie the knot a tug tighter.

We had the day off, unrestricted by the telephone or other distractions, and we dined elegantly, just the two of us, at an old, out-of-the-way hotel. Like newlyweds we ambled aimlessly through the little town, stopping at whatever caught the eye or heart, resting at last in a sweet shop where I bought the girl on my arm a strawberry yogurt cone.

For myself I ordered a treat I hadn't tasted in years, a rich strawberry ice cream soda. Ah, headier than champagne. How blessed I be to have a girl who understands this.

Then we were seated in the automobile again, heading back down the highway. No, not sadly, for the best was yet to come. We were going home.

My Greatest Generation

Greatest Generation? Maybe

You've heard it once or twice by now, the cogent observation offered by random observers that my generation ranks as this country's greatest. Roughly, my generation encompasses the men and women who existed during the Great Depression, who outlasted World War II, and who toiled to build a new world on a substructure of old-fashioned scruples.

It'd be foolish for me to dispute that dictum. Or at least it would've been so in my old madcap days. But not when you're married to an individual who has collected a couple of college degrees with honors. I wouldn't go as far as to characterize myself as having become a scholarly type, although more so than ever I do probe and question occurrences and tenets for deeper meaning. Handy example. Does "greatest generation" mean that ours has the largest membership? Or that perhaps we're the smartest? The prettiest? Holiest?

No matter how you size it up, word came out this week that the U.S. population of senior citizens is expected to double by the year 2030 to seventy million. That is, from 12.4 percent to nearly 20 percent of the population. Whew, that's a crowd of old-timers. Will the economy manage to support that many senior discounts? There—that's a new dilemma for the people who earn a living making government forecasts and recapitulations.

Between you and me, friends, I've never been knocked over by those unremitting deductions and rebates shamelessly framed to lure the older customer. I'm not about to deny that I do value matinee prices and restaurants featuring early-bird menus, but *those* perks are available to everybody regardless of age.

You know, almost any bystander can step forward and brand us the greatest generation, but have we lived up to our inborn responsibilities and obligations?

God only knows.

What kind of morality do we espouse?

Possibly the most striking lesson a generation can learn from war is that there are no atheists in foxholes.

OK, so then what?

Well, taking it a step beyond, I believe that when we the lucky returned from war and got back into civilized clothing, most of us tried our darnedest to trim away the crudeness and vulgarity accrued during the male-dominated undertaking. We yearned for a clean-cut meadow on which to love and honor our spouses, rear our sons and daughters, and we hankered for an honest day's work. Obviously a sizable number of us have a road to travel yet, but, so far, I think we've done our best.

Yes, all in all, I'd say, that as a generation, we're a fairly decent lot, born when three meals a day was a luxury.

We scrapped around, and we got a terrific kick out of living. For some, the big shootout came along and nipped our aspirations of higher education in the bud. We made sacrifices. We were quite good at that.

Some of us came back. Some of us were *so* lucky, we married college graduates.

Mother Teresa Would've Loved Harvey

It's become increasingly doubtful that Mother Teresa would've cut it as a mother superior at my grammar school. Much too lenient, much too forbearing. This, at all counts, is the conception after piecing together her saintly life, this Angel of Calcutta, the late torchbearer of the Missions of Charity.

Being called on the carpet in the principal's office at my first school was not a matter to be tossed off with shrug or juvenile bravura. Of course the most disagreeable part of the whole production, no matter the punishment dished out—one's parents were bound to get wind of the infraction, then legislate their own penalties. My memory divulges no occasion of outraged parents of that generation ever filing suit against the school over the ministering of cruel and inhuman discipline.

If indeed Mother Teresa had been occupying our principal's chair, her smile would've shattered the contemptuous sneer of the snottiest kid who ever walked in her door. It's the smile we glimpsed in the newspapers, the newsreels, the smile that illuminated a world.

Realistically, the nun would've been too fidgety for the academic chair at our parish school. The streets, the alleys, the dark doorways, those were her arena, scouting for beggars, the ailing, the tyrannized.

Shortly after her death, as the story goes, St. Peter himself turned her away from the Pearly Gates.

"Sorry, Mother, there are no slums up here."

Sister Teresa would've found supportive, charitable work aplenty in my old neighborhood with its oversupply of castaways of the Great Depression. Oh, and how she would've loved little Harvey.

Arriving at school one morning, after missing one too many meals, the seventh grader peeled off his winter coat in the wrap room, moaned, and hit the floor in a shocking, dead faint.

The only inheritance his impecunious, recently departed daddy had left him were work shirts—all of them too big. Today when I think of Harvey I envision him in the classroom or in the schoolyard habitually folding back the cuffs of those oversized denim shirts.

In the weeks following Mother Teresa's death, I retraced my footsteps in an effort to ascertain some measure of my own existence. And found it easy enough to be confronted by St. Peter at the Gate. There he stood, holding up his hand, saying, "Whoa, hold it right there, Edward."

Well, for one thing, he might've inquired if I recalled a boy named Harvey. And if ever I ventured to stand tall at his side, be his comrade, invite him home for a meal.

Count on this. Even before cooking a bowl of porridge for Harvey, Mother Teresa would've hugged his bony frame and tousled his hair.

In the end, the diminutive nun, easily lost in a crowd, stood head and shoulders above the universe.

Amen.

Case of the Missing Chapter

As an expiring sage once said, the inevitable is inevitable.

And so it came to pass last night here in my study. Chapter seventeen of the book I'm writing disappeared from the face of the Earth. Quicker than the snap of a finger. More exactly, when my forefinger pressed a wrong key on my computer.

Maybe it *was* inevitable after processing so many words, but down the drain went the words and music I'd painstakingly knitted and polished, gone forever.

Panic, temporary insanity, and devastation set in. I wailed for help, and my wife came on the run from her study across the house. Not only is she optimal when it comes to holding one's hand in time of crisis. Her mind is relentlessly analytical, her grasp of mechanical things far superior to mine. Alas, after thirty minutes of looking over my shoulder and tapping keys, she agreed. My twenty pages were kaput.

"I'm so sorry." Know what else she said? "I'd willingly lose everything I have stored in my own computer, if I could get those pages back for you."

What great love. Brought tears to my eyes.

All of the above makes for a good argument that maybe I should've stuck to my faithful old typewriter instead of buying a computer when I retired. But the debate loses steam when I remember the labor of typing and retyping pages and whole manuscripts. Nonetheless, now comes the onerous trial of rethinking in an attempt to repeat the missing chapter. Can I pull it off?

Don't forget, my old gray memory ain't what he used to be. Actually, I was *never* topnotch at remembering names, but not long ago while my wife and I were dining with a friend, I couldn't call up a certain word, an elementary word, and had to turn to her for help.

"What's the opposite of integration?"

How easily we forget.

And yet, all this could be worse. We imagine, wincing, how Ernest Hemingway must've agonized when someone made off with his briefcase containing the only copy of his entire novel.

My lone, lost chapter is out there in computerized orbit, and if it should show up on your directory, please contact me.

Factually, I've given up hope of finding it *in toto*. But every so often when a phrase from it floats across the screen of my memory, I quickly write it down. Clever as the computer is, it's not worth two bits to me in this recall—something I must do on my own. And that's gratifying in this age of computer dependence. Still, it *has* become a vital machine for me in collecting and rearranging words. But I must remember to work it alertly.

Even now as I come to the end of this piece, my finger hovers uneasily over the key that should connect the computer with the printer. If I do press the right key, these words will end up in your hands.

OK, let's try it. Ready? Here goes.

Presto!

One Too Many Doohickeys

In her middle to late eighties, I'd guess, a friendly sort—the woman standing at the pharmacy pickup window. She doesn't seem to grasp everything the pharmacist is explaining about her purchase, but she's into the spirit of the deal, smiling affably and nodding her head.

Now comes the part in the scenario where customers produce checks, credit cards, or cash. This woman withdraws checkbook and pen from an oversized pocket book. It seems a sound choice. She doesn't bear the appearance of an individual who moseys about parking lots and malls with a wad of cash in her bag. Also, it's possible that credit cards baffle her somewhat, particularly when she's expected to properly slide the plastic along the designated slot on the checkout counter herself.

Truthfully, I'm flummoxed by this maneuver myself. It's so simple, I know this, but I invariably do it backwards or upside down.

First time I ever put my card into play, I recall, the clerk quizzed me, "Debit or credit?"

She had me there. "Gee, I don't know," said I. "What would you suggest?"

Nor to this day have I ever paid for gasoline outside at the pump. Oh, I'm convinced I could ultimately get the hang of it, but I always pull in at the same guzzle stop, and do rather enjoy entering the store and tarrying with the proprietor and his hired lads.

My shortcomings are detailed here merely to point out that I'm writing about this elderly woman free of patronizing intent. Often when observing women of her lonely feather, I think of my own mom and I ponder, if she were still alive, how she might handle certain transactions and newfangled doohickeys on her own. It's doubtful Mom ever wrote one check in all her days. Her financial habits were coin purse and postal money orders.

Now the pharmacist proceeds to inform her mature customer that she need not write anything on the check, that the countertop machine will automatically fill in all the blanks.

Well now, did you ever hear of such a thing? If not flat puzzled, the woman is at least unconvinced.

"You mean all I have to do is write in the amount. How much is it?"

"No, we take care of all that," says the pharmacist. "All you have to do is sign the check. It's something new."

I'm not sure these are the words the patron necessarily wants to juggle at this point in her life. I study her face, the lingering, elderly smile as she glances over her shoulder, seemingly eager to share her thoughts with someone, anyone, as if knowing there won't be anyone home when she gets to her place.

Suddenly I have an inkling that she'd like to make a soft declaration about how easy companies make it for us to part with our money, but how much more fabulous it'd be if they could manage to make prescription drugs more affordable.

So I'm saying it for her.

Who're You?

In today's post there arrived a letter of singular curiosity from my wife's cousin in Colorado.

"How wonderful it must be," she writes, "to *be* something and *know* who you are."

She was alluding to my wife's calling as a storyteller.

"Here I am, sixty, and have no clue. I could tell you lots of things I'm not."

For the record, my cuz-in-law is retired from her job as a grammar school teacher, a not insignificant or ignoble credential. But she's a woman, who, for the most part, took things pretty much unquestioned as they unfolded in her life.

"As a youth," she states, "one is supposed to be searching for what one is. But I never did. Is there time? Do I need it? Do I just carry on?"

Yes, my wife *is* a storyteller, but this doesn't mean she knows all the happy endings. Nor does it mean that she walks around in our cottage small spouting interminable yarns. Or that she fabricates tales and conditions directed to maintaining a serene household for her husband.

Come to think of it, selfishly, that wouldn't be such an ignoble specialty, either.

My little storyteller for years has frisked her own soul, reviewed her aims in life, checked her orb. Pressed on by her other inherent proficiencies, is there some undiscovered commitment in which to invest her heart, some higher plan to attain? It's simply splendid, I dare say, that these two cousins and ex-roommates—and the many individuals like them at any age swimming around in the stream of consciousness—can take healthy, introspective looks into themselves and their world.

Who are they? What should they be doing?

After all, wasn't it Plato himself who said the unexamined life isn't worth living? Yes, I do think it was.

In truth it was my wife who passed along the old boy's quote. How blessed I am, mated to a degreed individual. Sometimes I wonder what she ever saw in me. All I have to show, dating back to the age of sixteen, is a doctorate of desire to write and to peddle entertaining words.

How about you, the reader of these chosen words today? Do you know who you are, who you're supposed to be? Do you know what you want or should be in this life?

Too many of us sitting over here in the senior section tend to dwell on who we *were*. And close our eyes to promising prospects.

No, it's never later than you think. And yet, still, even so, time does flutter by on wings swift and sure. Not to scare anyone, but you have taken note, haven't you, that the first wave of baby boomers has turned fifty?

If that doesn't stop you, make you think, as it does me, or if you just don't give a whoop about any of these questions, that's fine, that's dandy.

That's who you are.

Round and Round the Table

Eight of us sat around the round table.

Technically it was an oblong dining room table, but why haggle over adjectives? That's why poetic licenses are issued. The *effect* was of a round table, complete with quick, palatable conversation and rich grub.

The oldest person on hand, in his eighties, had a problem. His hearing. Most of the conversation seemed to be whizzing past him. Suddenly, his antenna wiggled and his eyes blinked alive when someone mentioned "VE Day." His frequency was tuned into those electric words all right. He'd been one of the boys over there on the day of Germany's surrender, and he wasted no time chipping into our dialogue with his two cents' worth. For him, all at once, fifty years were wiped away. But, said he, it wasn't all fireworks and *whooppee* over there. No, sir, not on your life. He'd soon found himself on an armed ship steaming toward Japan. Then, three days out to sea, word came that the world's first atomic bomb had been dropped—on Hiroshima. His ship instantly changed course and headed for the U.S.

"Oh, man alive," he said, "the greatest news I ever heard, the greatest ever."

As an ex-soldier I know the abounding, panoramic exuberance of his statement. At the time I was even closer to Japan, in Manila, preparing to invade. Of course, President Truman's intrepid decision to unleash the two cataclysmic, war-ending A-bombs opened a broad scope of debate, one that murmurs on today. Yet, if he hadn't decided to go ahead, would I have survived the invasion, lived to meet the woman who became my wife, or been privileged to sit at this table with her at my side?

My army outfit ultimately landed on Japanese soil, but as we waded ashore, not a shot was fired.

On this Sunday afternoon, as accountable individuals, we deliberated the human questions in the wake of Hiroshima and Nagasaki, although there was more going on here. Looking around the table at the three generations of us, relatives of blood and marriage, I wondered how many other families might be similarly occupied. We talked about the fiftieth anniversary of the big war's end, and about smaller wars, but we also had many other matters to hash over, less momentous, both serious and uproarious. What a cozy, fine time it was, at the dining room table, one of the solid anchors that tie family units together. The sealed circle, you might say.

My own circle reaches a long way back. How far? Can't pinpoint the precise date, but in deepest recollection I see myself eating supper with my parents and two brothers at the round wooden table, the centerpiece of our old kitchen. Everything seems to have emanated from that point.

And I have to smile, gazing back at that particular scene, because I see my eyes drowsily shutting, and my head bobbing around and about sleepily. If I fell asleep while eating, I must've been *very* young.

Bye-Bye, Blackboards

"*Era of blackboards ends.*"

My wife read the bold words to me, tweezing them from the front page of the morning newspaper.

"Aw, no, no, luv, say it ain't so," said I.

But I knew full well it was so. Only a matter of time, really, before it came to pass—if you believe old saws like "All nifty things come to an end."

To be upfront about it, I wasn't so dreadfully upset by the news. For example, it wasn't going to throw a monkey wrench into my retirement plans or anything half as catastrophic. Even so, for the greater part of my childhood I was encompassed by blackboards, thus they do occupy an alcove among my profound, tender—and, admittedly, a few not so cherished—recollections.

I at once suspected that the newspaper story, in some fashion, was directly hooked up to computerization, and of course I hit the right key on the nose. Nowadays what *isn't* computer compatible? The newspaper piece revealed that the University of Central Florida, a mighty fortress of computerized academia on the eastern outskirt of Orlando, has unveiled a $13.4 million building that features twenty-six classrooms, two lecture halls, and—now get this—not a single blackboard in the bundle.

Not even one *green*board.

Instead we find a plethora of network portals, wireless computer network servers, multimedia labs, and projection systems, including a ten-foot-high video projection screen, and so on. Ha. Listen to me, would you? Like I know what's going on with that inside technical info.

Lawdy, how it staggers the limbs when I think of the alp of words my mind snatched off a lifetime of blackboards, the stuff learned, all the trivia retained. And maybe the mistakes too? Well, isn't that why God made little erasers?

You had to be abidingly careful, however, not to be too swift with those erasers. One false swipe and your message was deleted evermore. Like pressing a computer's aggressive "*pffft!*" key.

How terribly young was I when my whimsical Uncle Willie had me believing that all the words and digits wiped off the blackboard were collected in an unseen basket somewhere, sorted, filed, and used again and again?

So now. Let's see. Do I remember the first chalked word I ever read in school? A wild guess is that was probably the name of my kindergarten teacher—may she repose in peace. Poor thing earned it.

Proceeding to poke around in the past, I can think of no sweeter extracurricular moment than being chosen to go out into the schoolyard to clean a box of blackboard erasers. Ah, yes, here it is, late of a breezy, spring Friday afternoon, the muted hum and the buzz of the school off behind me, and I'm standing alone, shirtsleeves and tie, padding the erasers together, the chalk dust trailing off with my dreams.

Life was simpler to figure out back then. Today, the handwriting is no longer on the wall.

Plainly a Good Man

*W*henever we sit around the table in somebody's kitchen and paw around in our family scrapbook of memories, my two brothers and I generally size up our departed dad in the framework of his antics. In short, his motivation to stimulate everybody's funny bone. He was a fellow who savored comic gimmicks and gadgetry, and jokes, practical and otherwise. He got more sport out of a bottle of stink perfume than a barrel of whiskey.

But there was another stripe to this man, I'm reminded, after reading a letter from one of my nephews.

"I'd like to know more about my family history," he wrote. "I vaguely recall my grandmother, but other than that, I don't have the luxury of grandparent memories."

Truthfully, I was cheered to hear from my youngest nephew and about this interest in the members of his family tree. Many of us, myself not excluded, wait too long to trace our ancestral trails. By the time we look around, there's no one left to ask about the empty limbs on the tree.

And how unfortunate for my nephew that he has no live impressions of his paternal grandpa, my dad. Sure, I can send off notes to the young man, but he's undoubtedly heard the stories from his own parents about Dad's gift for foolishness.

And suddenly, it's apparent that what I should tell him is this. Beneath all the waggery, underneath all the outrageous pranks, his grandpa was a good man and a sterling father. And he was there when needed most.

He died of a heart attack at sixty-two, a successful man, without a penny in his pocket.

Still, there's no denying he was a funny fellow, and that he handed down that strain to his three sons, one of whom just happens to be my older brother and this particular nephew's father.

Back in the days shortly after World War II, my brother always seemed to have a joke up his sleeve. Like the time he brought his newest girlfriend home for supper. I was in the back bedroom, and when my brother came in to fetch me, I was clad only in a bathrobe and trousers, having just stepped from the tub. He implored me to roll up my pants so they wouldn't show under the robe. The gist was for me to come out, and after the introduction I should exclaim, "Boy, it sure is hot in here." And then, to the shock of all present, suddenly whip off my robe.

Well, I was sorry to spoil his frippery, but I simply couldn't pull it off. Somehow I didn't think it the right foot to get off on when meeting one's future sister-in-law for the first time. He should've asked Dad to do it.

You know, my heart sags at the reminder that there are far too many little boys and girls around these days without a dad in the house, dads like mine—or dads like my two brothers, come to think of it.

Is This Trip Necessary?

So I said to myself, "Whoa, just a minute, big boy, is this trip necessary?"

Yes, I honestly spoke those words aloud, ignition key in hand, while parked at the front port of our cottage. And instantly the World War II catchphrase cut loose from the logjam of my memory, and flashed before my smiling eyes.

"Is This Trip Necessary?" That's what good old Uncle Sam wanted to know back in those lean, patriotic years, and his crucial message could be glimpsed here and there, on highway billboards, in periodicals. Radio comedians Bob Hope and Fred Allen, to name two, blended the subtle dictum into their skits. Charlie McCarthy kidded sidekick Edgar Bergen about the dubious necessity of his trip to the NBC studio that day.

Not surprisingly, the pitch never came close to the ringing popularity of "Remember Pearl Harbor!" but it did give Americans pause. Oh, and did we ever do some prime pausing and praying in that forbidding era. We hardly needed to be reminded that there was a war going on, but mainly the government was bent on making each citizen cognizant of the exigent need to conserve energy. Finally gas rationing did become a chilling fact of life in most parts of the country toward the closing weeks of 1942.

Today, certain social observers, fittingly or not, refer to my generation as America's greatest. Thank you very much, but don't think for a minute that there wasn't widespread beefing and whining about the distribution of those gas-rationing stickers that decorated car windshields. Personally, I thought the program was a grand idea, one more chance for everyone to pull shoulder-to-shoulder in the grand war effort. Besides, I didn't have a car.

The weekly allotment of gasoline, according to my rec-ollection, finally leveled off at four gallons per week for average folks with "A" stickers, and ten gallons for "B" drivers involved in essential service. The "C" crowd, clergy-men, doctors, and the like could swing in at gas stations and order "Fill 'er up" at will.

So was my trip to the strip mall the other day neces-sary? "Good question," I said to myself. And decided to put off the journey until the next day when I'd be on the road anyway. Returning to the cottage, I got a what's-up look from my wife. "Just a little gesture for the war effort," said I. Not to mention the skyrocketing cost of petrol.

Looking back, there seemed less grousing about the other elements of massive rationing: sugar, butter, meat, tires. Silk stockings were not rationed—but there were pre-cious few to be had. At one point, women painted their legs with makeup to give the illusion of wearing hose, then drew a line up the backs of their legs with eye liner for "seams."

I haven't heard of anyone lately who's painting on pantyhose.

All in all, my generation must've done something right. We won the war.

Early Bird Watcher

Stepping outdoors early in the morning is one of my elite recreations. Earlier the better. Between six and seven seems ideal.

The only span of my life when I did not care to rise up so early in the morn was during U.S. Army basic training. The reason for that was basic. Before peeling open one eye, I knew the day would hold absolutely no splendor for me.

Although I've been subjected to a profusion of vexatious alarm clocks in my day, science has yet to invent an awakening process more—well, more of an affront to mankind than a sergeant flashing on the lights and shrieking at the miserable, lowlife bleepers under his command to hit the floor.

But, in time, that too passed.

Ah, the sacrifices that one must make to bring peace in our time.

Most of my early-morning adventuring is limited to our front yard. The bigger back yard offers more possibilities, but I hesitate to intrude on the little family of raccoons savoring late-late suppers on the grapefruit and tangerine branches. And who knows what other animals or exotic birds might lurk in the weeded shadows of the lake? Also, one of the dogs behind the fences on either side might spy me and cry out a friendly good morning. Much as I value that, it could wake up the whole neighborhood.

Out front, before tooling around with the hose or sprinkler on God's little quarter-acre, I fill my eyes to brimming with sky. I don't stand there and try to be Robert Frost or somebody. All I do is salute the colors of the new day.

For a while I trample around the lot like the lord of the manor, and wave to the working class, to the infrequent drivers who steer by on our dead-end road to their jobs. My fondest wishes ride with them, hoping they find the surprise and wonderment that I once discovered on my daily downtown junkets.

Working couples with children live on both sides of us. One of the kids, a girl who needs all the fingers on one hand to tell her age, peeks through the hibiscus and brightly pipes, "Hi, Ed!" We live on a road with a future.

Then it's time to bend over to pick up the gift-wrapped newspaper in the gravel driveway, flip it high in the air behind me over head and shoulder, and if it's caught, that's a good omen. If it so happens that my wife is at the window, she might think I'm acting out another of my pre-breakfast superstitious rites, but superstition has nothing to do with it.

Some things work, and that's all there is to that. Like putting on the left sock first when dressing for the day or a date.

All right, now it's time to head back inside the cottage. There are things to do, promises to be kept. While it's still early morning.

It goes by so swiftly.

God Bless You

Now I lay me down to sleep. I pray the Lord *my soul to keep. If I should die before I wake, I pray the Lord my soul to take.*

Were you so blessed as to have learned this little prayer, or a variation, at your parents' knees?

Picture this: a freshly bathed child kneeling at the side of a bed, hands folded. "God bless Mommy and Daddy," and brothers and sisters if any there be, and maybe Grandpa and Grandma, and a few others who merit mention, a pal, a favorite teacher.

Simply astonishing, isn't it, to look back and count the few people it required to keep us clothed and fed, content and loved, to toe the straight and narrow.

One can guess that it'd be equally astounding to discover how many kids of the twenty-first century never heard this prayer. Or those who never experience the security check of the nightly tuck-in and a parent's kiss. Who have no one to talk to about their dreams, their deeds and misdeeds of the day—except for the dinosaurs dancing in their heads.

But then, yes, the years do whistle by, and our prayer list of names lengthens. Soon more people need our attention than the other way around.

You ever get the feeling at night or during the moments of daytime meditation, that you're leaving someone's name off your check-list of supplications? There's so much to hope and pray for, for us, our families, neighbors, a stranger who does us a kindness.

Naturally there are folks among us who don't believe in the power of prayer or feel the need to teach any to their children, or discuss the subject of moral values—if that term may be spoken without a lot of people rolling their eyes.

But that's OK. We have to do things our own way. That's what it's all about.

If you come across a better means of getting our country back on track, hop to it.

And listen, if I desire to privately pray for the well being of these doubters and their offshoots, why not? There's always room on my list to squeeze 'em in.

Someone recently asked if I still remember the "Now I lay me down" prayer we used to recite as youngsters. Remember it? I guess it's on the tip of my tongue every night, that's all. Good habits are hard to break.

Truthfully, there *are* a few slight alterations in my prayer nowadays. Goes something like this.

"Now I lay me down to sleep, and wouldn't it be wonderful if I could sleep the night right through? Even three or four unbroken hours would be immensely welcome. In any event, I pray the Lord my soul to keep. If I should die before I wake, and I really hope I don't because there are so many songs for me to sing yet—but if I do, *if* I do, I pray the Lord my soul to take."

Amen.

Where Art Thou, Cyrano?

Despite the poetic urge, I can't say that the fresh-cut, happy-yellow daffodils dominated the dining table. True, the bouquet was a resplendent touch. But when trappings outshine the grub, the possibility exists that I will leave the table feeling only spiritually nourished.

Such, happily, was not the case on a recent Sunday. Our table headliner was big-league lasagna, constructed of homemade pasta.

The vase of daffodils, however, did induce my wife into a dramatic, impromptu recitation of a poem while her married daughter, our hostess, cleared the table and readied the dessert. Aptly, the poem of choice was "The Daffodils" by William Wordsworth. Remember that one from your grade-school years? From the third grade in my wife's case. Astounding. You should've heard her. An enchantress.

"I wandered lonely as a cloud / that floats on high o'er vales and hills." So go the familiar opening lines of the four-stanza Wordsworth classic. And concludes: "And then my heart with pleasure fills / and dances with the daffodils."

Does that ring up any bells?

The piece got me thinking, wondering how many of us are walking around with unused scraps of old rhymes, perhaps full poems, hidden or rattling around in our heads? Can you recall any you were forced to memorize in school, and then had to stand up to recite in front of *everybody?*

I put myself to the memory test—and rather embarrassingly as it turned out. Here's the first poetic passage that leaped to mind: "Friends, Romans, countrymen, lend me your ears." It's pretty hard to bowl over anybody with a line of that sort today, or to introduce it offhandedly into a conversation. Perhaps the reason it remains emblazoned in my brain, other than its serious nature, is that it sounded so funny to my high school classmates the first time they heard it voiced.

Standing up front one day, a lanky kid croaked, "Lend me your ears!" And the majority of the room doubled over with giggles and guffaws. Now I ask you, how was I to pick up any culture, sharing classroom space with the likes of that primitive lot?

Oh, yes, I've always admired—and sometimes unashamedly loved—individuals who have a favorite poem, and can deliver it verbatim to round out the dinner mood of a fine Sunday afternoon.

Intermittently over the years I wished I'd had cogent, poetic reference material at my fingertips. Maybe to impress a mysterious, beautiful woman beside me at a party—the way it happens in movies and in books. In other words, to come on with the verbal moves of Cyrano de Bergerac. Alas, my repertoire was too threadbare for words. Such are the deficiencies from which fantasies are born.

In particular I remember a sensuous moment when recall of some proven romantic lines would've come in so handy, a moonlit moment that cried for a crowning of roses and violins. And so help me, all I could think of: "By the shores of Gitchie Gumee . . ."

Boomer Special Now Arriving

At breakfast I read the newly revised figures in the newspaper—seventy-six million baby boomers are crowding up to the threshold of retirement. That's a whole mountain range of fresh-faced seniors out there, ladies and gentlemen.

What excitement. What a cast. And it has all the earmarks of evolving into a smash production.

These days, in the event you've not been taking notes, more words are being published and uttered—more so than ever before in the history of the working man and woman—relative to the ways and means of getting the most jubilation out of retirement.

And that's good. Isn't it?

Well, I guess. But I should confess, every so often I do feel a pull of guilt that maybe I'm not holding up my end in Social Security's hurly-burly side show. Oh, I do keep busy, as the social events coordinators exhort us, no question about it. Still, have I consigned enough of my quality time to humanitarian causes? Am I achieving the utmost fulfillment of my own vast potential?

Gosh, this makes it seem like I'm just now starting out in life. Follow this arrow and before you know it, the retirement game seems too doggone cumbersome. Besides, confidentially, I don't see the necessity of taking on any unnecessary contrition.

As I sit here this day, balancing the profusion of all the available material—retirement advice, admonitions and data—I question if any of it is trickling down to grade-school levels? Is this so important? You're danged tootin'.

That is, if a recently published graphic is true. It shows a huge number of retirees cast into the lowest one-third of the social spectrum because they have the least education, the lowest expectations of themselves, and the paltriest savings.

It's hoped that this theme infiltrates the craniums of our little ones. Who knows, it could be the precise impetus that the beleaguered boards of education in this country need.

Naturally I wouldn't go around repeatedly singing the old refrain that it's later than the retired freshmen think. On the other hand, speaking from personal experience, retirement comes around *sooner* than the young men and women might think.

Even when voluntarily giving up my space in the time-clock world sixteen years ago, I was taken aback when retirement stole into my office one day, tapped me on the shoulder and said, "Are you ready? Let's go."

What it all simmers down to, I'd say, is that what retirees need more than anything is sheer luck. Las Vegas and lotto luck is OK, but I'm talking primarily about the fortune of reasonably good health. Please, dear fellow citizens, *please* take painstaking good care of yourselves.

Retirement is a grand place to be. Sometimes, admittedly, it takes a person a while to get accustomed to playing bit parts in the big show, but overall it's wonderful, it's marvelous, it's—well, it's one step short of heavenly.

Welcome aboard, boomers.

A Moment of Silence

I can still hear the silence.

On a midsummer's afternoon it was, and for the first time in my whole life I stepped inside a public library. Dressed in my best grade-school knickers and with my mom at my side, I'd gone to sign up for my very own library card. This was better than acquiring a driver's license. That's what I believed at the time, and nothing's changed my mind since.

Vaguely I recall the walk home then, and asking Mom why she'd felt it necessary to speak to the librarian in whispers. So as not to disturb the readers, of course. Well, sure, I could understand that much, except there'd not been one other soul present in our small, store-front, neighborhood branch on that vacation afternoon.

Actually, it took me some time to learn that libraries *demand* silence and hushed exchanges. And not only out of deference to readers, either. Shhh. Listen, my children, and you shall hear, the *murmuring* of all those books waiting on the shelves.

And my heart winces sharply as I ponder all the youngsters of today who might never tune in to that enchanted murmuring, or who might never catch those grand, old-fashioned, crispy silences.

Unquestionably magic carpets still park there, but something's not the same. I was especially aggrieved in recent days to read that in an expanding number of public libraries the hush is gone, that the shush has been flushed down the drain. Naturally, management at these stations doesn't invite young folks to run willy-nilly on the stairways and race through the aisles, nor does it condone any other kind of disruptive whoop-de-do. A way of putting it,

I suppose, is that libraries have transformed into community clubhouses.

That's about it, my friends, a location where individuals and families hang out together to be amused or take part in cultural programs. In itself, that's not atrocious. In fact, it's the type of enterprise that gets my impassioned vote. With only one stipulation. That this culture be carried out behind closed doors. In a soundproof room.

Silence, as everyone knows, is golden. At least we knew it once upon a time—in our schools, houses of worship, libraries. Say, come to think of it, a few decades have come and gone now since last I saw a sign posted on a street near a hospital alerting motorists and pedestrians that they'd entered a quiet zone.

Today, so it seems, decibel by decibel, the silence of our planet is being suppressed, almost to the point—without stretching the point—of landing a slot on the *golden-oldies* hit parade.

Although none of this should be taken as a volcanic matter that's been festering under my cap for a long spell, I did feel moved on this day to say a few words in behalf of silence. A so-long salute, if you will, to an old friend.

Please, bow your heads, and let us observe a moment of it.

A Toast to the Milky Way

Some kids had to be warned to "finish your milk."

When pouring from the bottle at *our* thrifty kitchen table, Mom had to measure each glass scrupulously, making sure that not one of her three little sons had grounds to grumble about getting gypped. Or so she revealed to us in later years.

Milk was vital to the daily diet of boys and girls. Everybody knew that. It was as crucial as downing eight glasses of water a day, sleeping eight hours a night, and enjoying a luxuriance of fresh air and exercise.

Now comes word via the media that a faction of medical practitioners is questioning the nutritional merit of milk. And get this. It might even be detrimental for some children.

Wait, we're talking here about cow's milk, right? Not goat's milk, not coconut milk, correct?

One doctor was quoted, "There's no reason to drink cow's milk at any time in your life."

Aw, say it ain't so, doc.

Once upon a time I thought there was no keener after-school snack than a few of Mom's icebox cookies, washed down with a nice little glass of ice-cold milk. I still think the coupling of pie and milk was made in Heaven.

My sister-in-law recently baked two apple pies for my younger brother's birthday dinner, and after she humbly accepted the assembly's standing ovation, I pressed her for the secret of her picture-perfect browned crusts. Before sliding her pies into the oven, she said, she rubs the crusts and tops with milk-dipped fingertips. "I learned that little trick years ago from your mother."

Tell you this. To drink water instead of milk with pies so sumptuous, well, it borders sacrilege.

I don't contest the proposition that an infant should drink only its mother's milk during the first year of life. On the other hand, perhaps for old-times' sake, my sympathies lean to the dairy official who claimed it "unsound and nutritiously dangerous" to advocate that kids stop drinking milk. It's an argument we can expect to hear more of, producers and watchdogs preaching their translations of the truth, one more dietary direction to confuse consumers.

Meanwhile, my intention is to keep drinking milk, although by my doctor's edict I have scaled back to skim milk.

But, then, I'm only a shadow of the heavy drinker I once was—as when, for example, I worked in a retail dairy store. One day I knocked off a half-gallon bottle of homogenized at lunch. Of course, back in those days, decades ago, my lunch box contained four sandwiches, a piece of cake, and fruit.

In January of '46, Red Cross workers in Seattle greeted our returning troop ship with a carton of milk for each soldier. Nothing could've been sweeter, more symbolic. The good old U.S. stretched before us with a future of believable virtue.

Maybe we expected more of it, as it turned out, but, oh, it's still grand, this land flowing with skim milk and honey.

Mugged or Hugged?

Mugged. Now I know how it feels.

Well, first, let me explain that I make a habit of keeping a dollar-bill handy in my pocket, rather than digging for my wallet when approached and addressed by a drifter. Is there anyone among us these days who's not familiar by now with the clever old saw that says it's plain stupid to flash one's cash and cards in front of a stranger? Secondly, it's flustering to finger through one's cash for the smallest denomination while the slope-shouldered itinerant stands before you with tongue hanging out.

Now this is not to say I'm a patsy for any Tom, Dick or hustler. I'm a cheapskate, and I readily admit it, when it comes to sharing my retirement funds with the bloodshot, aimless, milling masses.

It still registers as a shock to me—surely to *any* faithful, Depression-disciplined soul—when a panhandler steps up and seeks "a dollar or two." A "little extra change" was all they solicited not long ago. And, really, not too long before that, the battle hymn of the republic was: "Brother, can you spare a dime?"

Over the years while strolling through the park, and ambling our downtown streets, I've heard just about every tale of misfortune and misadventure that moochers can concoct in pursuit of untaxable income. But I prefer to pick my own charity cases, often without the exchange of a word. I measure the vagabond by style, that's what I do, by his or her smile, sobriety, any sincere attempt to look presentable in the company of others.

Example. On a frosty morn downtown a few months back, I passed an unshaven, gentle-faced bloke of middle age in an oversized, recycled overcoat, sitting in the sun on the steps of a closed church, reading a newspaper. I'm impressed by readers of newspapers—and never mind if it's been rescued from a trash barrel. I went back and offered the gent a dollar so he could go buy a cup of coffee for himself. Bingo. I could see it in his eyes, I'd hit the jackpot. A cup of warmth had come his way, and he'd been spared the ignominy of begging for it.

Now. To the recent case. I dug into my jeans and gave the handy dollar bill to a forthright young dude with evident, reasonable needs. He glanced at the bill, and almost came apart at the seams with gratitude. Pumped my hand over and over. Thank you, sir, thank you, kind sir.

That night at home, emptying my pockets, I came across the dollar bill. What the—? What gives? Then it hit me between the eyes like an exclamation point. That morning, meaning to stop at the service station, I'd also slipped a twenty in my pocket.

I'd given the guy *twenty bucks* instead of the *single*.

Truly I felt I'd been mugged. But it lasted a mere moment—until I put myself in his shoes, in the shoes of a beggar.

Hello, You're On the Air

Embarrassed? Yes, that was the dominant emotion of the moment. After all, my cohort from the newspaper and I were not exactly unknown personalities in central Florida. And there we sat, at live microphones, earphones in place, on a talk show in the studio of an influential radio station. The only problem: no listeners were calling in.

This was back when I was still pulling down a workingman's paycheck—my Edwardian years, as I like to think of them—specifically during my tenure as book editor. Our host, Helen Pekin, a grand old dame of the air waves (may she rest in peace), had invited Hartwell Conklin and me to share half an hour with her in regards to our upcoming gala, Dinner with the Authors. My sidekick was the producer of this annual literary banquet—featuring three major writers and staged at a swank hotel—and I the interlocutor; but half an hour is a long time to entertain people on the air, particularly if there are no commercials, if you've come prepared primarily to answer questions, and, worse, if you can't sing.

During most of my time on this planet I've considered myself a better writer than orator. Strewn about in my field of daydreams, however, are instances when I believed my creative skills lay beyond writing—acting on the stage, for instance, or in films. In my teens I was profoundly influenced by Orson Welles and his *Mercury Theatre on the Air.* I recall writing and narrating a script in his style. A friend recorded it for me on the equipment in his bedroom. Alas, I'd not been born with Welles' elegant vocal resonance, and listening to the playback of that record was like getting hit with a weapon of artistic mass destruction.

Sure, there were other times later when I still dreamed—as most of us Muggles do—of addressing vast audiences and holding them spellbound. Actually, serving as MC at Dinner with the Authors gave me a taste of it: the magic of audience esteem. At one show—and I utter these lines in whispered humility—my opening brought down the house. Believe me, that moment has buoyed me for nearly 20 years. Often in the shower I replay the scene, pretending the rush of water is the roar of the crowd—the way some blokes might fantasize about fanning Joe DiMaggio, Hank Greenberg, and Ted Williams in the ninth inning of the All-Star game.

Anyway, just as my associate from the newspaper and I were running out of questions to ask ourselves that afternoon in the studio, we received a call. Ah, yes, finally, *finally,* oh, thank you, *thank* you. A male voice. Obviously of intellectual stripe. He asked pertinent questions about the banquet and deliberated the guest authors' works. Best of all, he got personal: He'd been following and admiring my writing in the paper over the years.

Then, as we chatted merrily on the air, his voice began to sound vaguely familiar. Before he hung up, I was certain. The caller was my brother.

Would You Say That Again, Lord?

I whispered, *"What? What'd he say?"*

"I'm not sure," my wife whispered back.

The preacher's key phrase, in a singularly meaningful oration up to that point, had been engulfed by a cacophonous cough from the pew behind us. And I engaged in an instant skirmish of self-discipline at that point, in an effort to keep myself from from swiveling around haughtily and firing off a direct, scalding, shaming glare at the offender.

It's possible the fellow might've just been powerless, you see, to catch the cough and murder it in a handkerchief as it sneaked up on him like a sudden summer sneeze. And, who knows, the man might also have been victim of a lingering ailment.

In this instance I'm reminded of the story told about John Barrymore, and how he reacted in costume on stage when someone on the other side of the footlights began coughing. Even though the guilty party tried valiantly to suppress the annoyance, the actor stopped in the middle of his triumphant soliloquy and shot a vicious visual arrow at him. Hard as the poor soul tried, he couldn't stop hacking, but he did reach down to fetch his two crutches and went hobbling pitifully up the middle aisle and out the doors.

In church as well, we have the chronic, chafing listeners out there in the congregation or audience, those who arbitrarily decide to cough or clear their throats at awkward moments. Granted, a portion of these actions are legitimate, such as an individual's determination that a certain sermon is ranging tediously out of hand.

Then, not to be overlooked, there are the nose blowers. Oh, yes. They, especially those of the trumpet-blare sort, would seem to have more chance for self-control, and yet a few of them rank right up there with the disrespectful hackers.

Unlike some individuals, I've never been able of to create much racket when blowing my nose. One of my grammar school classmates sounded much like a tuba when applying a hanky to his schnoz. He got a laugh and a big hand every time. Never missed. Once, trying to mimic him, I nearly blew my adenoids out.

By the way, did you catch this headline in the newspaper? "FBI warns of hacker copycats." Oh, wow, I thought. Didn't realize the problem was *that* threatening. But a sub-headline explained that the FBI was hot on the trail of *computer* hackers.

I'm not suggesting that each utterance that disturbs the spiritual peace might result in the loss of one damned soul. Even so, awareness and sensitivity in the matter of coughing or sneezing or unwrapping lozenges would be hailed.

Picture this. I'm present, meekly, at the Sermon on the Mount, and I hear, "Blessed are the meek, for they shall—" And the remainder of those immortal words are swallowed up by somebody's unthinking, rip-roaring, free-wheeling cough.

Flustered, naturally, I turn to my wife and whisper, "What? What'd He say?"

All Aboard

We saw a friend off at the railroad station several days ago. Haven't done that in years.

Usually when my wife and I bid provisional farewells to old acquaintances, relatives, neighbors and house guests, the performances take place on the gravel driveway of our cottage. Or, perish the thought, it entails a lengthy drive across town on our well-used boulevards and along the specialized touch-and-go trails that zero in on our spectacular, sprawling, swarming international airport.

Our most recent goodbye was staged on nearby Winter Park's open, intimate Amtrak platform.

Despite bum weather to the north and bum weather to the south, the engineer sounded the horn no more than a few minutes late as the train coiled into view around the south turn of tracks. Ah, such a grandiose sight. There she was, the gleaming, beaming, one-eyed, friendly monster aiming directly in our direction. I do believe a chill would've slithered down my spine even if I'd not been caught up in an untypically sunless Florida afternoon.

True, I do miss the classic train whistle of bygone days, the faraway cry of the old steam locomotive, but, clearly, something important was taking place on this stage, someone was going somewhere.

The bell was clanging on the illuminated crossing signal on the street behind the small-town station, the train grunted to a halt, and the self-possessed conductor swung down. I swear I smelled cinders.

Our friend, ticketed for New York City, was appropriately bundled up for its typically brutal February weather. If imperative he had to go off, we wanted to go with him. He wiped away a tear. In truth he wanted to stay, but he was on a mercy mission to be at his ailing mother's bedside.

Later, motoring home, I reminded my wife that entirely too much time—four or five years—had elapsed since we'd last taken a choo-choo ride together. Idly she wondered if I could remember riding the rails for the first time ever.

Oh, my dear, yes, sixty years ago, a run of only a few uninspiring miles, Jefferson Barracks to Union Station in St. Louis, where I changed trains to the war. The antique station has since been transformed into a world-class festival marketplace, or so my older brother tells me, but on the screen in my head, I suppose, it'll always be the world's biggest and busiest railroad station.

Lord, yes, I can still hear the continuous, high, monotone of information echoing from the loudspeakers in the heat of those peak wartime years, and all the jabber, laughing, and crying you can stuff into one dramatic production.

Our friend might not get to sniff the daisies, but traveling by train, or bus, for that matter, you *see* it, the whole bouquet.

And then he was gone, and we stood there, and all we heard was the faint, fading clickety-clack echoing back.

The Pub, the Fireplace

Entrenched at my desk, I glance left and salute the boys. They always make me smile. They never change, never ask anything of me. Lovely group to have around. The men in the photo, the four of them, unmistakable Irishmen, range from young to middle-age.

My wife snapped this shot of us—that's me in the middle—in Ireland a few years back. I had it blown up and mounted for the wall of my study. It's one of my prized possessions now, a photo that holds forth about the size of a window, opening into the world of my forebears.

My missus and I had been in London for a week that year, and on the flight over to Shannon Airport, we struck up a dialogue with a priest. His sister would be picking him up and he offered us a lift as far as Limerick, if interested. Ah, the Ireland of the Welcomes we'd been reading about. Afterward, by taxi, we traveled the remaining winding miles, thirty minutes or so, into Killaloe on the River Shannon.

Following breakfast at our hotel the next day, Sunday, we hired a driver to take us a few more miles in the hinterlands to the village of Ogonnelloe. And there it was, the church where my dad had knelt and prayed as a boy before sailing to America.

Practically next door stood the pub, only slightly remodeled from the old place my grandparents once owned, and where they raised their family. If only my dad could've been with us. With a family of his own to rear, he'd never gone back. Once he received a letter from his closest boyhood pal, Tim Lynch, who told of hearing of some Americans arriving in Killaloe. With a singing heart Tim had hurried in to see if it might be his old chum—only to return home monumentally disappointed. A few years later I wrote to tell him that my dad had died.

And so my wife and I attended Mass in my dad's church that Sunday morn, in his memory, then visited the family pub. You must believe that when I stepped inside those storied premises, my emotions were in a spin and my eyes filling up. Although the serving of libations would not be officially permitted until noon, the new landlord welcomed us with a smile as wide as an Irish countryside mile. Anyway, four customers—the lads of my photograph—had already gotten a jump on the starting bell. In no time at all, as they poured out the tales I ached to hear, we were old friends.

Today here in my study, Christmas at hand, the season that cries for remembrance and the nearness of cherished ones, I wish more than ever that the boys could step out of that photo and into our American home. I'd love to show 'em my town, have them meet my family, my neighbors. Oh, and wouldn't the blarney flow like the Shannon.

Before my wife and I withdrew from the pub that day, I stood by the fireplace where my dad's mom always sat rocking after a long day's labor, puffing a clay pipe, sipping a hot toddy. How many Christmas Eves had she sat there, the old woman, staring into the embers, knowing in her heart she'd never again see her son, or ever lay eyes on *his* three sons?

Acting My Age

Do I feel any older? It was a question tossed at me on a day most recent when I turned seventy-eight.

My reply: "Actually I do, yes." Might's well be honest. Not a day goes by that I don't feel a wee older. And wiser? Actually, that, too, yes.

And while at it, I suppose this particular banality should also be stated: I never expected—at least not in my more audacious years—to reach this elevated age. Or anywhere near it. There was a time when I nursed the ominous feeling that I'd not live beyond thirty-three, but after clearing that hurdle, I stopped messing with the guessing.

No, the above foreboding had nothing to do with the war. Oh, by "the war," plainly, I refer to World War II, the one into which I was drafted as a teenager. And it's worth mentioning that I was a soldier with absolutely no fear of death. Of course, this probably had something to do with the fact that some high-ranking gaucho in the Allied war machine declared that I was not cut out to be a fighter pilot, commando, or infantryman. Even at that I got shipped overseas.

Now that's when I began to worry some. Frankly, that's when I lost my devil-may-care attitude for good.

Anyhow, when it comes to longevity, about the only guessing I do nowadays is measuring the age of others. These seasoned people, the men and women I covertly size up in public—are they older or younger than I? That's what I'd like to know.

Did anyone at any time ever call them cute?

Not that all this makes a whisker of difference in the long run, but it's a drill I've fallen into.

What I'm really wondering, I reckon: Do I look my age? I recall my mom once telling me to *act* my age. I was ten or so, and whimpering about some triviality. Since then, no one has upbraided me to act *or* look my age.

When word leaked out recently in a diner that it was my birthday, and a server coyly inquired how it felt to be thirty-nine, I informed her—in a steady voice, mind you—of my real age.

"No!" the worker gasped.

But I couldn't tell if that single word and exclamation point was another way of saying, "Oh, you poor man!" or "You certainly don't *look* that old!"

If the latter reaction could conceivably be true, it's possible that when making entrances with my wife on my arm, I give the impression of being younger—because of the gap in our ages. I'm not so foolish as to divulge my wife's age, but will say this. At one point in our relationship, if I'd gotten fresh with her, I might've been branded a cradle-snatcher.

Aw, it's a wonderful life, all and all, but no matter how you look at it, and even with age discrimination outlawed, it's a youth-accented world.

I should know. I helped build it.

Our Three-Alarm Specialist

Digesting the last remnants of breakfast—
egg substitute and a genuine bagel—I hastened through the
house to see who was out there pounding on our front door.

Turned out to be a next-door neighbor, a psychothera-
pist by trade, a gracious fellow, in the early stages of middle age. This day, uncharacteristically, he had a mildly wild
look in his eyes as I flung open the door.

"When did this happen?" he said, raising a section of
the morning newspaper in his fist, as though asking if he
was in time to help put out the fire.

Evidently he'd just read my column, an account of how
I had witlessly allowed my computer to devour a chapter of
the blockbuster book I'm writing.

Of course, by the time he arrived, the fire was out, so
to speak. I'd already recuperated from a bout with despair,
and after an intense week's work, had actually reconstruct-
ed the lost pages.

Confidentially, they might have improved. At least this
is what one assures oneself after suffering the mental and
physical pangs of reconstructive surgery. But the neighbor
had rushed over to see if he could help retrieve the missing
twenty pages. Who could ask for anything more?

"Same thing happened to me a few years ago," he said,
"except I lost my entire dissertation."

Apparently all users have horror tales to tell.

But he had managed, with expert aid, to piece the frag-
ments of his doctoral document back together. "If it happens to you again, don't touch anything. Call me."

I'm only one step above computer illiteracy, so think
what it means to have a virtuoso for a neighbor.

This is the same man who rushed to my aid earlier this

year when a malicious wind tore a brawny limb from our cedar tree and nearly impaled me. Shaken though I was, I put to work at once to clear the branches from the road. In no time at all the neighbor and his twenty-something step-son, unbidden, were on the scene with saws, and in less than an hour the road was open to traffic, the branches and logs cut and neatly piled. It's a scene I recall whenever his dog wakes me at 5 A.M.

After he went home the other morning, I wondered guiltily if I'd been as kind to all the people who've lived within the sound of my voice? I'm no expert in anything, but had I been too stingy with my time and interest?

Later, our neighbor returned, bearing a gift of software to help my wife and me remedy future computer gaffes. He inserted the disc into her computer. Explained its use. She peered intelligently over his shoulder.

But I stood back. And I nearly cried, because I realized how lucky I was at my age to be living in this place, to be mated to this sagacious woman, to have such a caring neighbor, and because I didn't understand a word he was saying.

Trip to the Field

Something my wife said today before breakfast. Let's see now, what was it? Oh, yes: a line lifted from the newspaper, an item regarding a school field trip. Yep, that's it.

For some unexplainable reason, those two little words—field trip—activated my funny bone. Leastwise, that's what I call this bone of emotion that sends me stepping off to all sorts of funny, captivating places.

Frequently as I stand in the kitchen filling our favorite cereal bowls, my wife skims the day's newspaper and relays headlines calling attention to wars and rumors of war and endless bureaucratic chicanery. Possibly, at that specific moment, I was especially hungry to hear something different, words of perhaps extraordinary global insignificance.

As for the field trip itself, I wasn't filled in on the dates and details, but that part of the story is irrelevant. I felt a spurt of pure gladness for the boys and girls immersed in it, or any such extracurricular adventure. How stimulating it must be, in the middle of a school day, to close the books, and with your heart picking up the beat, march out into the world at large.

We never had any of those perks or educational pick-me-ups at our parochial school. I'm skeptical that the public schools in our general neighborhood boasted any either. To my recollection, only once in my time did our student body venture off the hallowed grounds during regular hours, and this was a solemn hike of several miles to a church event. It would've been asking a bit much of us if we'd had to tramp that distance with our hands prayerfully folded. Even so, our deportment was stringently monitored, so it couldn't have been much of a *whoopee* outing.

If it'd ever come to pass that our principal felt moved to instill hard-core contemporary reality into her scholars, she might've organized a tour of the city poor house. I *assume* such an institution truly existed. Certainly we young ones heard this dirge often enough around our homes: "If things don't get better, we'll all end up in the city poor house."

Well, the reality I glimpsed with my own two juvenile brown eyes was a colony of penniless people, boys and girls my age and their parents, living on a strip of cardboard shanties dubbed Hooverville, along the Mississippi River levee.

But there were survivors. Oh, yes, many came back alive from the Depression jungle, and we went on to constitute a great generation.

Today, my heart splashes over with hope for our young, born in a world spinning crookedly. Fear rules. There's no longer safety in numbers. You remember the busload of kids in Israel wiped out recently by a suicide bomber.

I want our lads and our lasses to have their field trips, their computers, small classes, and teachers good enough to sign bonus contracts—and all the rainbows they need.

They're the next greatest generation.

Not the Worst of Times

MISSES AND HITS: ON THE WINNING SIDE

My Pet Story

Once upon a time I had a dog. And a big, brave animal he was. Even though he's been sadly out of the picture for quite some time now, I still hesitate to speak or write the name to which he once so faithfully answered.

You know how that goes. My guess, there's not one person among us who doesn't have at least one personal recollection along these pet lines.

I still know the sinewy feel of the big fella inside my hug, the only dog I ever called my own.

One day, back in another time, when my longest pants were short pants, my dad brought home a puppy. For some baffling reason the minuscule mutt favored me from the litter of us three little brothers to bark at, to chase menacingly up and down the yard and nip my heels. Listen, I dashed around in circles almost that whole day, doing a bit of howling myself, and by sundown the feisty newcomer had been taken back to a neighbor and returned to his mama's side.

Anyway, a lifetime later, when illness wrested the life out of my best pal, my dog, several well-intentioned folks counseled me to bring a new pet aboard immediately. While this philosophy and therapy might be just the ticket for some pet-devotees, I was no longer in position—or *willing*—to invest affection, time, space, and emotion in another canine sidekick. My attitude has not modified since then.

So, does this make me a one-dog man?

Let me put it this way. I'm piously praying that no one leaves a surprise basket of joy on my doorstep on a Christmas morn, or at Easter, or for my birthday, thank you.

The only other dog to work its way into a position of loyal attachment in my heart was a shaggy Lhasa Apso named Buckley, belonging to a young woman in our family. I have to divulge this with some pride that it was I, fourteen years ago, who suggested she name the dog as a salute to William F. Buckley, Jr., a master of words whose writing we both esteemed in that period.

Now our story fast-forwards to several weeks ago, to the young woman's chance for a career move to San Francisco. But what to do about her beloved Buckley? By this time the poor little critter was blind, deaf, and barely mobile. Leave him with relatives? A vet advised against shipping him by air. OK, she'd take Buckley along in the car.

"I'll die," she said, "if Buckley dies along the way."

Well, they made it OK, they sure did, just the two pals, motoring Monday to Friday, Florida to San Francisco—2,600 miles. I'm told that Buckley was quite restless along the way, but he hung on tenaciously.

What no one needed to tell me is that he knew, somehow, that he *must* get his mistress to her new city where she could get a fresh start in life.

Next morning, he died.

Booklover's Nightmare

This is not the worst of times. It does seem that way, though, doesn't it, at times?

'Tis the season for rampages, major and minor. You can check it out in the morning newspaper or catch it on the evening news on the telly.

My favorite bagger and resident clairvoyant over at the supermarket solemnly predicted that mankind and womankind could expect plenty of funny stuff to occur in the coming days, as we drew within sniffing range of the twenty-first century.

As my friend the oracle so quaintly phrased it, "People ought to slow down because nobody's going to get there ahead of nobody else."

Then there's one of my lettered neighbors who suggests there'll be widespread simmering down when the last hurricane of the season blows out to sea and dissipates.

Yeah, yeah, and maybe this and maybe that.

Truthfully, I doubt the weather regulates our country's stifling political climate, although, admittedly, as of right now, there's nothing going on in Washington and in a certain state capitol that a breath of fresh air couldn't remedy.

Some of us citizens who've been shuffling around this land of ours for multitudinous years tend to string along with the concept that there is much more monstrous conduct afoot in today's world than we generated or encountered years ago. If not, we certainly *hear* more about it. Nothing is left unreported, and the nonstop scrutiny of it burdens the soul. You can't tell the saints from the sinners without a scorecard, folks! That's the sales pitch.

And yet, confidentially, it's not the rampages that keep me awake at night.

Like wars, like rumors of wars, we'll always have among us frantic-eyed legislators, self-destructive families, assassins, and terrorists. True enough, but when these misguided mortals struck in the past, let it also be known, and with no uncertainty, that there wasn't a dry eye in this house of ours.

Today's tastelessness. That's it. I think that's the cut that gouges the deepest. Yes, the fact that crudeness too often has its way, that civility is in short supply.

One night this week, I took a novel to bed, a book deposited on my doorstep earlier that day—one of the cultured services provided by our downtown public library. For weeks I'd been anticipating reading this book, but after turning a mere half-dozen pages my heart slumped.

No, I was not floored by the foul word appearing before me. Lamentably, today one must overlook such boorishness, even from some of our literary heroes.

The page had been desecrated by the previous reader. That's it. Instead of using the new invention called a bookmark, the cheeky perpetrator had *actually* folded over the page, almost in half, to mark his or her place. The entire, practically new book was indelibly and unfeelingly sullied in this fashion.

No, this is not the worst of crimes. It only seemed so, for a time, to one booklover the other night in bed.

Anna and Rose

Instantly I recognized the pair of young women in the old photograph. My mom and her younger sister, my Aunt Rose.

Actually, it was a little more gripping than a simple matter of identification. Here's what happened.

My wife entered my study yesterday morning with a computerized enlargement of that old snapshot, and it was as if Mom, my own *mom*, had physically walked in with her. It hit me that dramatically.

For quite a number of years now I've had a fairly enduring picture of Mom tucked away in my noggin—the face from the last decade of her life. Even in my own later years, when daydreaming myself back on a trip to boyhood, this was the face of Mom that usually surfaced.

The mind's a tricky arena. A daydreamer can go only so far within its borders. As an example, it's virtually impossible to convince myself that I'm eleven years *older* than my mom ever was. Fact is, I'll always be looking up to her.

So, when my wife showed up in my cove yesterday, I was hardly ready to meet the person she brought in with her, this tall, slim, healthy, dolled-up woman. So young, so elegant.

Where were the gnarled, arthritic hands, the obvious curvature of the spine, the threadbare gray hair?

It should be pointed out that the original photo, shot in or around 1927, is in the possession of one of my St. Louis cousins, who recently came across a duplicate in his collection. He then passed it along to my older brother who still lives in our old hometown. Within minutes the picture was winging electronically, Missouri to Florida, and coming to life clearly on the printer in my wife's study.

She's the only person in this shelter, by the way, who has the accouterments—all right, and also the wherewithal—to handle such miracles as this.

Miracle, marvel, call it what you will. I'm sure Mom and her little sister would've been all skimble-scamble had they known that their picture would one day attract so much notice.

As it is, they pose formally side by side in front of another sister's house, as if harboring doubts that the Brownie in the unseen photographer's hands will truly perpetuate their likenesses.

Aunt Rose isn't wearing a flowing gown, but from the flowers she bears it's conceivable that the photo was snapped on her wedding day. Both babes are outfitted in chic dresses with fashionable, low-slung sashes. I don't remember my mom ever looking so fetching.

Oh, yes, the sisters have been preserved. They never made the headlines, but they should've gone peacefully to their graves insured by the awareness that they'd been faithful, loving wives and mothers.

After the camera clicks, I picture the sisters relaxing, laughing, and hugging, then turning up the wooden steps to the porch and into their sister's house to rejoin the merriment.

Excuse me now as I follow them in.

The Hot Corner

Seated in the aluminum bleachers ringing the diamond, it's hard to tell precisely how old the players are. Mid to late twenties? There's something about donning a baseball uniform that makes a fellow look older, harder.

I recall putting on a baseball cap, possibly my first, at age nine, and darned if I didn't look ten or more.

Baseball players spend lots of minutes inspecting themselves in mirrors before stepping out on the martial turf—pants tight, tucks just right, all that. Yes, and the cap must sit just so on the skull. Although caps are crucial to protect the players' eyes from the sun and their hair, they also come in handy to tug and nervously readjust while the boys are standing around on stage waiting for something to happen.

OK, here I am, a Sunday afternoon, watching a congregation of baseballers, and all I can tell for sure is that they're here on this barbarously hot day for the uncontested love of the game. Why else? Only the two umpires get paid. Not much glory to be handed out either because the scene is a high school field near downtown Orlando, and the stands are deserted—except for a few players' wives and children. And there are no squinting, big league scouts on the grounds expecting to sign hotshot prospects.

My presence here was dictated by invitation only. Sort of. No one offered me a uniform and the chance to join the fracas, but a friend nonchalantly disclosed that he'd be playing third base for his club today. Third base? The hot comer? At his age (thirty-nine's my guess)? This I had to see.

In the first minute, walking from my parked car, I knew I was in the right place. I couldn't whiff the hot dogs or the peanuts and Cracker Jacks, but I could smell *baseball.*

Long ago, not far from this site, say about an 880-yard

runaway, I covered the Minnesota Twins in spring training and the Orlando Twins during the summer. Also, I'm reminded of the magnificent weekends when my little brother and I would go watch our big brother pitch—before he joined the navy. Often our mom and dad would be among the onlookers.

And now here I am, feeling almost unpatriotic for being away so long. Oh, that's my friend over there, the one guarding third base and tugging the bill of his red cap. This is no old man's league, but he's the oldest on the field, and guess what? He smashes the ball for a single to left, and steals second off a kid with a Winchester arm.

Still, I advise him to hang onto his nighttime job: managing an award-winning seafood restaurant. I look at him, and the other boys out there, and at baseball in its shiniest hour. It's a carbon-copy scene, played coast to coast. Crowds or not, it's still baseball—the fun, same discipline, obeying all the rules, and somebody's keeping score. Here, everybody's an all-American.

Fiddling Away the Time

My guess, one of these days Daylight Saving Time will be history. As in *buried* history.

Maybe you've taken notice that some citizens are getting increasingly steamy under the collar about the system annually foisted upon them. Why bother? That's what they'd like to know. Is it worth all the foofaraw? That's the kind of explicit language the conscientious objectors are slinging around.

On the other hand, if there are just as many persons around who *delight* in an evening's extra daylight, I wouldn't be at all incredulous—except I don't hear much from them. This bloc accepts matters as they are, and that's that.

I see myself pretty much falling in step with this detachment, even though if it actually came to a showdown, I'd more than likely throw in with the crowd backing standard time across the board.

First of all, on a long sweltering day, I dearly fancy the idea of a cool, calming early dusk.

Of course it was radically different for the beautiful people of my set in the 1920s and 30s. No summer day was too long or too torrid for us. We pinched and saved just about every inch of fun-loving daylight we could lay our hands on.

Come to that, the soft evenings weren't so hard to take, either, for those of us who were allowed out after dark. We had all those engrossing games by gaslight, and for the hand-holding boys and girls there were lanes to walk, down where trees hid the street lamps.

Ah, yes, yes, sweet yesterday, but back to today.

By and large I'm an early riser, and even in retirement I truly and ambitiously anticipate the first inspirational crack of dawn.

Daylight Saving Time, designed for the maximum use of seasonal daylight, quite obviously, burst initially upon on the American scene during World War I to conserve fuel. Did the private citizenry raise a stink about it then? I can't say. My close contacts from that era, God bless 'em, have passed into the eternal time zone.

However, I do recall my dad speaking strong words against the reestablishment of DST in the era of World War II. "Tinkering with the natural order of things." That's how he felt about it, adding, "Is it worth all the foofaraw?"

I don't know, but without this questionable procedure, we'd be deprived of some pretty funny stuff. Well, like the poor souls forgetting to set their clocks ahead and sashaying into church on that Sunday morning as everyone else is going home.

DST also gives occasion, unbidden or not, to count how many timepieces we have strategically scattered through our houses. At our place this year, before going to bed on the eve of DST, my wife and I had sixteen clocks and watches and other timed apparatuses to reset and fiddle with. It was like one of those old war movies, the two of us shouting across the house to synchronize our watches.

Talk about foofaraw.

Take a Bow, Aunt Mary

Hardly a boy or a girl existed in my day who did not have an Aunt Mary.

And so on this day I slow down for a few moments to ponder why Mary, that sweet, grand old name, has fallen from grace in recent years when it comes time for mamas and papas to christen their newborn darlings?

These days, the place I'm most apt to see the name, sorry to say, is the obituaries page.

Does this mean that one day soon there will be no more staunch Aunt Marys hovering out there to love us, counsel and coddle us, to just *be* there?

From time to time, for various reasons, newspapers publish photographs of children, but it's been a long spell since last I noticed a little girl identified in cutlines as just plain Mary.

Offbeat, exotic, hard-to-spell, hard-to-pronounce, creative names, that's the hot ticket. Nothing particularly improper about this practice, although it does smack of tastelessness and irresponsibility when, say, an entertainer who publicly struts indecently, might name her daughter Decency or Purity.

At any rate, Aunt Mary showed up in the headlines recently. No, not *my* dear Aunt Mary. She never did anything so consequential as to warrant a headline—except, perhaps, for a simple notation over her death notice. This was Mary Moody Emerson, aunt of Ralph Waldo. That's right, as in Ralph Waldo *Emerson*, one of the idols of American letters.

If we are to believe a certain individual of academic caste, there is the distinct probability that Ralph Waldo, who preached, "Trust thyself," actually pinched some of his material from his aunt. Evidently the purposeful Mary Moody wrote a letter to her twenty-one-year-old nephew in 1824 in which she opined:

"Solitude, which to people not talented to deviate from the beaten track (which is the safeguarding of mediocrity) without offending, is to learning and talents the only labyrinth (though sometimes gloomy) to form eagle wings which will bear one farther than suns and stars."

Oh, boy, with a jawbreaker of a paragraph like that to guide him, little wonder that it took Ralph Waldo thirty-six years to pen his famous essay, "Culture," along the same lines.

My Aunt Mary once ribbed me for recommending a novel to her that sported a call girl in its cast of characters. That's about the total sum of our intellectual affinity. But I loved going to Aunt Mary's. A lush plum tree stood just outside her kitchen door, and her house had a built-in warm scent of plum pastries, and there was always a jar of plum jam in the cupboard ready for uncorking.

Confidentially, I think Ralph Waldo Emerson's Aunt Mary would've been overjoyed that she helped in any small way to polish her nephew's literary star. Aunt Marys weren't created simply to smile back at us from old photographs. Certainly she wouldn't have sued her nephew, or raised a stink about it in the tabloids.

Aunt Marys don't do stuff like that.

A Little Girl Comes Home Again

One of the girls who once lived in this house came back to spend a few days under our roof. And it was good.

It wasn't her first visitation after a dreadfully elongated absence. No, nothing quite so dramatic—nor melodramatic, as such affairs have been known to unfold.

She's changed. Naturally. Folks who knew her only as a winsome, reserved small person, would scarcely pick her out from a band of other beautiful, well-versed women today, especially beyond this domestic setting.

Oh, well, yes, maybe the technicolor burst of flowing auburn hair could be a giveaway, plus the quick, penetrating eyes still brimming with all those little secrets. But today she stands on her own, erectly, as the discriminating woman she's chosen to be. That's the crux. If anything, then, she's more herself than ever she used to be.

Sitting cross-legged on the floor of our living room opposite a drop-in, former college classmate, she said, "This was a good street to be brought up on."

And my wife's heart did sing. Oh, did it ever. She's been periodically nagged by the likelihood of not having provided her two daughters with a more enchanting environment.

Actually, it's *still* a good street—a short dead-end road fenced with grandfather oaks. And yet it's a long enough stretch to bear an interesting crook down a ways toward the middle, and enough families—back then in particular—to beget a litter of prime playmates.

Imagine the rapture, a little girl wandering alone from this house and discovering a friend close by who loves mysteries and the Nancy Drew books as madly as she. And who's game to become an active partner in the formation of a detective agency.

"Did we have any *cases?*" The young woman laughed mockingly at my absurd question. "Of *course* we had cases."

Listen, didn't they nail the culprit who pilfered her bicycle from right here on our own property? And wasn't there a full cadre of shady characters in the neighborhood to keep an eye on, to shadow from oak to oak if necessary? However, the old case file on the swiping of another of her bicycles—from a padlocked stall at school, mind you—still has her baffled.

On the night this week when the young woman went early to bed—she had an early flight to catch—she slid into bed with a mystery novel. But she left the guest room door ajar, in the event, presumably, someone cared to stop by to chat.

From the kitchen I looked down the hall at them, the mother and the daughter conversing together in the soft light of one more goodbye. And I marveled at how much alike they were, and also how beautifully individual—each her own woman.

And it was good.

And Into the Pressure Cooker

Our home was invaded one day by a pressure cooker.

From whence it came, I can't say. That is, I'm unable to recall who gave it to my mom, or on what occasion. Probably a gift at Christmas. Maybe Mother's Day. Her birthday? Possibly.

This unequivocally: It *was* an occasion. Goodness gracious yes. An *event*. Presumably it was our family's first interaction—not counting the telephone and bathtub—with modern technology.

Now *there's* a term to curl my gray whiskers.

When it comes to modern technology, I don't mind harvesting the benefits, and exploiting its breakthroughs for a better way of life, but don't expect me to fathom it.

I compose on a computer, the straightforward word processing side, and that's it. I'd prefer not listening to anyone defining the intricate, extracurricular tricks at my command, or to tell me to throw open the windows.

I think my mom, who was born too soon, might've enjoyed puttering about with computers—once she got over the awe and implausibility of it all. Remember, here was a woman who beamed like the sun when she came into possession of her first genuine, pop-up toaster. Though not a lettered individual, she always looked a mechanical problem straight in the eye. Let's say the toaster, or a lamp or an iron, went on the blink. She'd dig out her screwdriver, friction tape, and pinchers, carefully take the appliance apart, then put it back in tick-tock order.

Too often nowadays, recalcitrant equipment ends up in plastic garbage bags, or hangs on for new life in somebody's garage sale.

Of course we must also remember that these gadgets in my mom's day were superior to those of today, and well worth saving. That is, if we subscribe to the all-American assembly line hypothesis that nothing manufactured today is quite as durable as that from the old days.

The pressure cooker was a different kettle of fish. The thing surely looked durable. Scary, too. It came with instructions for the user to practice extreme caution when cooking. Sure, I guess so, with all that pressure and steam building up inside the airtight pot.

Yes, the lid was also equipped with a little escape cylinder, and the first time we saw it popping and spitting with pent-up vengeance, we all backstepped out of explosion range.

"Turn it off, turn it *off!*" cried my little brother.

On hands and knees Mom crawled to the stove, and with her head down she reached up and turned off the gas. But she refused to be browbeaten by a household appliance—like her two sisters—and eventually felt comfortable with it. How much time it saved her is a moot point. The dear woman was conditioned to spending half her life in the kitchen anyway.

It might've been different had she lived to see the coming of microwave ovens.

Well, neither gadget would've *improved* her cooking. Modern technology could never catch up with Mom in that.

Free Delivery: Love

$\mathcal{S}$*uddenly there came a sharp rap-rap-*rapping from the front of our modest residence.

Emerging from my study in a dressing gown, I tracked down a round, beaming face peering in at me through the little fan-shaped windows of the door. Unhesitatingly I flung it open.

Laden with bags, the uniformed caller cried, "Hi!"

She then proceeded to inform me that she was the bearer of good news—in the form of ready-to-devour victuals "from your tender, loving daughter!"

My wife had spoken to her older daughter less than an hour before on the phone, so naturally the mother felt a warm spurt of tears over this bombshell presentation.

Is it possible there were also few drops in my eyes? I'd say it's conceivable, yes.

At any count, here was the young, vivacious assistant manager for a local branch of a national restaurant chain bearing three brawny, lined food bags. This restaurant doesn't normally deliver its goods, but as my wife later gleaned, her daughter pleaded for an exemption with the manager via long-distance phone, on the grounds that her parents were in their late eighties—a forgivable exaggeration—and just home from the hospital.

Actually, my wife *had* been taken to the emergency room several days before after a freak fall in the house, and had submitted to surgery, and was now ensconced at home for seven days with her wounded knee propped up.

Gently stacked in the bags, as I swiftly sniffed out, were a meat loaf, an alp of sliced turkey breast, roast chicken, vegetables, mashed potatoes, gravy, corn bread, a Dutch apple pie, and a hummingbird cake.

That night, unaware that Santa Claus had come nine months early to our domicile, my wife's bosom friend drove up with a cooked pork loin roast, small roasted potatoes, mixed vegetables, salad, rolls, fresh fruit, and slices of coffee cake.

"I'm sorry," she said, "you'll have to mix the salad yourself."

"Hmmmph," I whimpered on cue.

Seriously, I had earlier welcomed the opportunity to do a bit of showing off in the kitchen while my mate mended. I'm no Emeril, but neither, after all, am I a complete ignoramus in that division of the house.

True, the food presently piled up in our icebox—including toothsome leftovers of smoked turkey breast, sweet potatoes and a spinach souffle, gifts from a neighbor—all had been precooked. Still, it takes skill to figure out a fitting menu, and to properly warm up each dish, and bring it all together seductively, at the same time, for snappy serving to the patient.

Honestly, the way our cup runneth over, I've been feeling—well, almost guilty. Please understand, I'm talking now about the abounding flourishing of love, not foodstuffs.

Oh, excuse me. There's someone at the front door.

OK, I'm back. You're not going to believe this. It was a young woman, a stranger. I swear, I have no clue who sent her, but she smiled and said, "Hi, here's your *pizza!*"

The Man with the Pipe

Not once, while seated at the keyboard this morning, did I reach for the pipe in my mouth. Because it wasn't there. And hasn't been there for about, gosh, going on seven years now. But do I still *miss* smoking a pipe? I do, yes.

Oh, yes, it'd become such a habit that even in the days shortly after deciding to stop, I could still feel the stem clenched between my teeth. And frequently thereafter, when writing a column or a story, I'd reach for it, and wrap my fingers around the inspirational, aromatic bowl—that wasn't there. It'd been part of my creative tools for 50 years.

I'm not sure if I would've had the mettle to simply stop cold one day. What happened, I'd endured major surgery, and after coming home from the hospital, did not resume the habit. Now, whole weeks, even months go by without my relegating any thoughts to my pipes, or to the full, four-teen-ounce can of Half and Half tobacco on a shelf as close as the reach of my long right arm. This morning, I remembered all. Ardently.

Halfway into breakfast, I turned my newspaper page, and there it was, the lugubrious news that my friend Sloan Wilson had died. Most of the book-reading world remembers him as the author of *The Man in the Gray Flannel Suit*. In my mind he rests in peace as the assiduous pipe smoker. And I say as much, not knowing if he even stoked up any of his pipes in the last few years of his life. He'd been suffering from Alzheimer's disease, and died at 83, in Colonial Beach, Virginia, on the last Sunday of May, '03.

During the 1980s, before departing Central Florida to fulfill his dream of living on a boat, he logged time as a writer-in-residence at Rollins College, and became a feature cast member of the literary scene here. I recall a fellow employee at the newspaper telling me that at a party the previous night he'd been in the company of "Sloan Wilson and his stinky pipe."

When you invited Sloan, you invited his pipe. Both were always welcome in our home even though normally my wife enforces a no-smoking restriction. Did that include me, master of the manor? No, sir—as long as I puffed in my study or on the sundeck.

Sloan left a profound vacancy when departing the area. He was affable, accessible, quick with calorific laughter. It wasn't always easy, being the author of a novel whose title is engraved in the American lexicon. So many disciples pressed close to hear his familiar recitations. Couldn't have been easy either for Betty, his wife and constant companion, sitting in on all her husband's reruns. But as she confided to my wife one day, "Who listens?"

I wouldn't mind stepping out on our sundeck now, and relaxing with Sloan in the gloaming. We'd just sit quietly, the two of us, each smoking one last pipeful.

The Artless Dodger

"*Down with dodgeball, down with dodgeball!*"
I knew a goodly number of individuals a few years back who would've been tickled to go parading in school yards with placards championing a crusade of that sort. And these males and females weren't all haughty types or scaredy-cats, either. Evidently, according to the newspapers, there currently is a groundswell of intensity in parts of the United States to do away with this playground game. That's right, *ban* it.

In all fairness, though, there's probably an equal number—possibly more—academics and phys-eddies willing to go down swinging and kicking in an effort to retain the recreation as a tool to teach kids the joys of competition, survival and agility. These are vital skills, they point out, for everyday life for almost everyone—steering shopping carts up and down the congested aisles of supermarkets, just one example. Actually, I didn't have to saddle up on a safari to find a passionate anti-dodgeball voice.

"I hated it," said my wife, "all those people who wanted to pursue me and hurt me and laugh at me. Years later it's all I remember about the silly game—if you can *call* it a game." *Humiliation* was another word she vented in subsequent mutterings.

Ostensibly, of course, the objective of dodgeball isn't to hurt or humiliate any player. Even at that, someone once expounded the theory that the game was dreamed up to give classroom oafs an above-board chance—during recess on the playgrounds—to get even with smarty-pants types and teachers' pets. To upgrade their low self-images, in short. So much depends on the kind of ball put into play. In my time inside the dodgers' circle, I felt the stings and arrows of tennis balls, softballs, handballs, volley balls, soccer balls, footballs and snowballs.

But you know, no matter how soft the ball—beach ball and spitball not excluded—if thrown with enough snarling, smoke-eyed rancor, it could have serious traumatic side effects for the victim. However, truly, on the face of it, dodgeball doesn't qualify as deleterious amusement, in particular when you consider the possible alternatives. Supposing, for instance, my wife, as a girl, would've been delegated to participate in tackle football or pole vaulting.

Granted, the mood being what it is around so many schools today, maybe we don't need any recreation that presents additional traumatic dilemmas for our boys and girls. But as for humiliation, it's always been with us, certainly where two or more kids are gathered. Yes, even in action as rudimentary as choosing up sides for dodgeball, or any game.

Clearly I recall the drama of getting to play in a softball game on the brick street in front of our house. The two captains took turns picking players, looking us over like sides of beef. I also remember how it feels to be picked last.

Now *that's* humiliation.

Tune It Down, Please

We little rascals, both boys and girls, gave little thought to the melody of the music blaring at us as we sat stuffed into those motion picture shows.

The musical score reached out from the silver screen, lassoed us, and swept us along on the frenzied chase over the hills and through the valleys of the untamed West.

Traditionally that's the way the matinee feature or serial opened, somebody forever chasing somebody, usually on ponies. The music was loud, louder than thundering hoof beats. Moviemakers knew the volume had to be tuned up in order to be heard over a standing-room-only audience of howling juveniles.

So what's their excuse *today?*

Increasingly, at cinemas and while watching television, my artistic sensibilities are stampeded by distracting background music. Well, it is distracting to the point of drowning out the dialogue, that's all. It's almost as annoying as taping a TV film, only to find out that it ran well beyond the advertised time.

True, some of the unrefined words that infiltrate pictures today *should* be drummed-and-bugled out, but, unfortunately, the profane always seems to eclipse the sound of music.

A lifetime ago when I was knocking on theatrical doors and just plain knocking around in Hollywood, the picture industry conformed to an unspoken artistic yardstick when it came to background music—exclusive of the made-for-matinee movies, of course. The ideal musical score, simply, was the one the audience was unaware of hearing during a quality movie.

That's a tall order. It still works in many cases, but over

the years, the overall picture has changed. A plethora of lush original music has been stacking up in the archives, much of it instantly identifiable with particular films. *Dr. Zhivago* and the moody whodunit *Laura* leap to mind. Also, there's much do-re-mi to be made now in the recording industry with the sale of movie soundtracks.

All I ask—*beg* for—is a common-sense mix on the screen. Automobile tires squealing, trucks smashing into walls, buildings exploding and imploding, damsels in distress screaming, space vehicles zipping and zapping, are abrasive enough. But even these seldom trample on the crucial spoken word.

I rest my case.

By the way, while on the subject, did you ever imagine that you're starring in a film, say while at home alone going about your chores? Or at the workplace? Did you hum, sing or whistle your own background music as the imaginary cameras rolled? What theme did you select, or *would* you pick for yourself, you the star, in all your glory?

Along a downtown avenue this week, I pictured myself walking to the theme of *High Noon*—firm-jawed, square-shouldered, long-striding, fearless, resolute, admired.

Suddenly, to my right, I caught the reflection of that man in a store window, keeping in step and staring at me. Only thing was, he looked more like Gabby Hayes than Gary Cooper.

Piggy-Back Penance

Had there been a handy label such as "cruel and inhuman punishment" back then, surely my pal Rudy would've pasted it on his forehead that day as he rumbled home from school, grumbling all the way. All he had to do before rumbling back to class next day was eat supper, sleep, have breakfast, and find time to write "I must behave myself in class" three-hundred times.

At his house he turned to Raymond and me, his cohorts in our unholy eighth-grade triumvirate. "Come on in, boys, let's get started."

Raymond and I exchanged sharp edged glances. Let us get started? But we trailed our friend in need up the run-down wooden steps, and entered. His mom, out shopping, had left him a Polish sausage sandwich wrapped in butcher's paper in the icebox. Chomping on it at the kitchen table, he ripped two sheets from his Big Chief tablet. Atop each paper he wrote his "I must behave" penance, then passed the pages around. Our mission: Fill in the blank lines below, imitating his hand. Meanwhile, after licking his fingers clean, he'd fill in pages of his own. "We're all in this together, right?"

Confidentially, it was news to Raymond and me that we were all in it together. I didn't even know how Rudy got in this pickle in the first place. Being good sports, though, we did give our buddy a hand. Truth is, we weren't cut out to be forgers. After an exacting fifteen minutes our documents were too bogus for words.

That's when Raymond hit us with his brainstorm: "Do it piggyback!" Placing one pencil on top of another, and fixing the points just so on the paper, he demonstrated how Rudy could write two lines simultaneously. Although it's doubtful that this high-tech cunning originated with Raymond, I was quite impressed. Rudy? Ecstatic. Sure, when the tactic was put in motion it proved pathetically awkward, yet the simple fact that he was putting one over on the teacher booted him along.

Newspaper ads and stories today remind us that school vacations are nearly ending. And I muse: Will any children have reason to employ the covert piggyback writing style? Probably they've never heard of it—all computerized things considered.

I also think of friendships the kids are about to renew or fashion. Ah, if only I could reveal that Raymond, Rudy and I became lifelong buddies. Alas, we drifted apart. I did see Rudy seven years later when my Army outfit caught up with his mangled infantry division in New Guinea. Poor guy looked twenty years older. But for me it was a transforming meeting. Silently, after all those years, I forgave him for not offering anybody a bite of that Polish sausage sandwich.

Three Coins in the Hanky

When we three little boys left the house on a trek of some sort, together or alone, our mom always made sure that each had a freshly washed and ironed handkerchief tucked into his hip pocket.

This was vital not only for smart dress and hygienic functions. Coins to cover the total cost of our outing were also knotted into the corner of each hanky for safekeeping.

Sometimes the toughest challenge of this whole production was trying to untie Mom's rigid knot to get at the cash when needed.

"Don't lose your money!" was one of her called cautions as we'd head up the alley toward the streetcar loop.

Not much chance of that happening unless we got a little too cute and started waving the hankies over our heads or out the window of a moving trolley.

Let's say we were bound for a mid-July baseball game at the magnificent Sportsman's Park, the city's baseball cathedral. The attraction of the day: our beloved Cardinals vs. the Brooklyn Dodgers. Boy, just the very thought of that flammable match-up—Gas-House Gang taking on Dem Bums—was enough to curl the hair on the back of any scrawny neck.

Anyway, this meant that my two brothers and I would need three nickels apiece to get us through the afternoon. Now you can see why so much effort was spent on security. Forty-five cents for three pre-teen boys embodied quite a spending spree in the '30s.

Of course for us—card-carrying members of the Knot Hole Gang—there was no admission charge at the ballpark. One of the nickels was earmarked for a treat, either a Popsicle or a chocolate-coated ice cream-on-a-stick, about midway in the game, or maybe during the seventh-inning stretch if anybody could hold out that long. The other two nickels were *carfare* to and from that sweet field of teams.

Carfare. Ah, now there's a word to latch the imagination, to shake the dust from, and to take a second look at. Makes me speculate as to how many boys and girls in today's sleek days of vans and carpooling know what the word means, or ever heard it spoken.

Can it be found in dictionaries? Well . . . yes, here it is in my Webster's: "The price of a ride on a subway, bus, etc." That's OK, but why is *streetcar* omitted? Wasn't *carfare* derived *originally* from those old conveyances? Have even the scholars down at Webster's forgotten?

Then, too, there was this caveat from Mom as we made tracks for the carline: "Don't forget to ask for a transfer!"

That's right. Miss the connection with the rollicking trolley that ran right up to the ball park and you'd end up downtown somewhere—with only a nickel left for a sad-faced trip back home.

But the last of our mom's reminders as she stood waving goodbye at the alley gate covered everything. "Be careful!"

Yes, ma'am. 'Bye, Mom.

The Stranger in My Study

Propped on a bookshelf beside my desk is a new photograph. New, that is, to the gallery of my treasured photos, paintings, posters, icons, and company. This newest addition is the product of a professional portrait photographer, the picture encased in one of those neat, old-fashioned, economical holders that unfold into a standing frame.

Back in another time, one could find rows of these formal photos in their serviceable frames, standing at attention on pianos, end tables, and mantelpieces in almost anybody's living room or parlor or—as we called it at our humble little house, front room.

The frame I'm looking at today reveals a young man, a stranger, wearing a uniform of the U.S. Army.

The print was mailed by one of my cousins in Missouri "for safekeeping." He's been thinning out his baggage prior to moving into a condominium. Admirable of him, but how much niftier it'd been if he'd desired to hold on to the photo for old times' sake. After all, the soldier happens to be me.

Yep, 'tis I—the January '46 version.

When I said the soldier was a stranger, what I meant, there's been quite a passage of time since last I looked in the mirror and saw this twenty-one-year-old stripling. It's taken a few days to reacquaint with him, but there he sits, fittingly, on a bookshelf, lanky legs dangling down—or so I imagine.

He's smiling and seems to be saying, "OK, world, the big war's over, here I am, back from over there, and ready to make my move."

The sudden appearance of the close-up photo gave me a chill of reality. Pinning my shoulders back in the swivel chair, I braced for the conflicting, inescapable waves of nostalgia and lament. I had wildly promised this young man so much, so many worldly prizes, spiritual trophies.

And then I remembered a haunting line from a Betty Ann Weber poem. A woman in her middle years is gazing upon a framed photo of herself as a little girl. The girl looks back and guilelessly asks, "What have you done with my life?"

Ah, there's a question to knock anybody's socks and sneakers off, regardless of age or foot size.

Oddly, a few afternoons later, I received another ripe photo, this one from my older brother—our parents' wedding portrait, with a request I fill in the name of Dad's best man.

Julius, my godfather, came immediately to mind. I dispatched the data on the evening mail coach. Now, after giving it more thought, I'm not unconditionally positive about that identification. Wish Dad was still alive so I could ask him. A kid really should know the name of his dad's best man.

OK, so here I sit in my gallery, in the valley of laughs and tears, and I hear the soldier boy whistle at me. Our eyes meet. I know *his* name. I still have hopes of making some of his better dreams come true.

Back at the Golden Gate

Fifty-six years had passed since last I winked at the Golden Gate Bridge. And for a breathless moment I felt all the tears and all the laughter and all the love that have rippled under the poised landmark.

This was several days ago at Fort Point, I moseying mist-eyed as suspicious waves snipped at my heels—beneath the almighty arm of the bridge, remembering.

My mom and dad were still alive then—two-thousand miles and half a century away from this point—and after they waved goodbye to me they went back inside our home and settled in, waiting, praying for my swift flawless return from another part of a wounded world.

It'd taken an open-windowed troop train three days to chug a bunch of us in natty Army uniforms into orange-scented California. In another few days we were aboard a ferry, followed by squadrons of shrieking, hungry, mooching seagulls. Sometimes I think the Army uncaged those birds strictly for our entertainment, and perhaps to short-circuit our sensibilities from the bludgeoning reality that we were about to scale the gangplank of an unescorted troop ship.

And now here I was, back in San Francisco, the year 2000, a willing visitor this time around, my wife beside me, and her daughter—a high-techy in residence—our fast-stepping tour guide.

One evening we walked from her flat to Fort Mason, and from a bluff we could look down on the port of embarkation. And once more, for a minute only, I was a tall, skinny teenager lining up with a drove of other helmeted, back-packed strangers, slightly dazed, knowing nothing about *anything*—except that we were booked for a perilous, unknown port.

I don't know how much I know *today*—the two women in our San Francisco party didn't press me for dialogue on this revisitation, possibly deducing that I needed time alone to sort out my post-World War II emotions.

Was this the moment to glance back on my life and quiz myself—where did I go wrong?

Well, hold on, just a minute now, what made me think I *did* go wrong?

True, in '46 after taking off my uniform the last time, I did vow with bravado to follow in the literary footsteps of William Saroyan, once one of the prominent cave-dwellers here. But if I fell off the wagon and pared my own path, was that an unpardonable sin?

Anyway, the Golden Gate Bridge is the centerpiece— in this city that looks like a familiar movie set—and from there we visited all that time allowed along the roller-coaster streets.

Late one afternoon our guide treated us to a fancy high tea at the St. Francis Hotel. That night, all night, we heard the moody foghorn. We also stopped in a shop called City Lights Books. Saroyan, Jack Kerouac, Thomas Merton, and other luminaries hung out here.

With some bravado I winked at all their ghosts.

An Outside Job

Unseasonably cool. So said the weatherman for sunny central Florida.

"Ah," thought I, rubbing my hands together, "here's the chance to try that procedure sent in by a reader."

Please note, the hand-written instructions for the routine, mailed by a woman in Grand Forks, North Dakota, were difficult to decipher. Mind you, I'm not carping about it. Goodness gracious I'm not. I'm tickled that the eighty-seven-year-old reader, burdened by macular degeneration, took the time and exerted the patience to write at all.

Truthfully, her handwriting is more legible than mine, and I have no alibi—not a kid of my age, and who'd been strictly tutored in school with the Palmer Method. For years I was aware that my retrogressive penmanship had irked my late Uncle Fred. He possessed one of the finest hands in our clan and once quizzed my older brother as to where I'd gone wrong.

All that aside, my pen friend in upper Dakota was evidently fired up by one of my weekly columns, the one in which I weighed the yearning scent of burning leaves. And she desired to share her long-standing, nostalgic routine of keeping warm.

At first I didn't know quite what to make of it when a double sheet from the *Grand Forks Herald* slid from her envelope. It'd been folded and scissored, so that a round hole appeared in the middle of each page. Presumably the fundamental concept was to warm the paper at the stove, then place this "hot news" against the skin beneath one's underthings, sweater, and jacket or coat before going out to plow the snow across the bitter northern landscape to school. At least this is the snapshot my imagination took.

One point, however, wasn't clear. Should I place my head through the hole, as a football player might don shoulder pads? Or, since I'd been sent two openings, plunge an arm into each one? I chose the latter strategy, first laying the papers over a hot-air register and turning up the thermostat. Thus padded, I was ready to go out and hit the exercise trail. Oh, the weather outside was delightful for the early-morn experiment, the temperature having plummeted to a bone-chilling 58 degrees.

Well, in the end, folks, frankly, I failed to convince myself that this warming technique was worth the bother.

But before writing back to the woman I retrieved her letter, and in a brighter light read it again, with a magnifying glass. Thank goodness, because I missed a few crucial particulars in the first hurried reading, and it's mortifying to say so.

OK, I was right about warming the papers, but slipping them under one's duds was only a temporary move—while plowing through the snow to the *outhouse*. That's right: what I walked around with under my T-shirt and sweater the other day were outhouse seat covers.

What else can I say?

I had the warmest armpits in Florida that morning.

Land of Free Laughter

She said, "I think I'm going to cry."

That's what someone very dear to me said this very day.

To be honest, I didn't feel too awful about it. Not that I'm the insensitive type. I'm as susceptible as the next fellow to anyone's melancholy, whimpers, and sniffles. Maybe a notch or two above the average, frankly.

Regardless, I didn't feel too terrible about the foregoing disclosure because it wasn't dispensed by a damsel in distress. If there *had* been something dire in the works, the tears likely would've preceded the spoken emotion.

Please note that I'm not here engaged on a fault-finding mission. Actually, I think—and I speak strictly from personal experience—it's OK for an individual to indulge in an occasional quiet cry. On whatever grounds. If only for the reason of sitting alone in the gloaming.

Still, if given the choice, I'll take a laugh over a cry any hour of the week. Ah, to laugh or to cry? That's the query too many of us too often thrust before ourselves on our daily wanderings. And you know what? It's understandable. Absolutely.

Grief, as you're sorely aware, is the hot commodity of the day. Good Lord, will the terror and horror never taper off? Obviously I have no insider information, but before this paper lands in your hands, it's possible our country will be at war. Oh, the abomination. And the quiet crying could well rise to the level of uncontrollable, heart-twisting wailing.

Even so, despite all the rampant hostility and boorishness, despite even the loss of the space shuttle *Columbia*—laughter is certain to prevail in this country. That's our genius. We have the gift to laugh at ourselves and *with* each other. The ongoing realization of this fact, at my age, continues to flabbergast me.

Do you have any concept of how many times a day you laugh? Keep count sometime. You'll be surprised.

Uncle Fred was the illustrious laugher in my relative circle as a boy. And, man, how easily he did succumb to my juvenile jokes, insufferable as they must've been. He wasn't loud, but he'd throw his head back and open his mouth wide as he could, and out would come the moist mirth in a great exhalation of breath, sounding almost like a wheeze— of hurricane force. His laughter is his monument.

Oh, the power of it. Quick example: a babe in a cradle looks around and suddenly laughs, and a group of mature onlookers breaks out in a severe case of giggles and coos.

Maybe some of us don't feel up to jocularity right now. That's OK. We take our knocks, and sob, but the laughter's bound to bounce back again. To smile, to laugh, is faith.

Oh, say, can you believe how lucky you and I are to be living in the home of the brave, and the land of the free laughter?

So lucky I could cry.

Why Me, Oh, Lord?

Why, oh, Lord, why me?

That's my wail of a question today. Why have I been singled out? What have I done to deserve this sort of treatment?

My hair and mustache are tattletale gray, I can't zip from bed in the morning with the same zing of my back-yonder days. I sit on the side of the bed, collecting myself, waiting till the ticker hits a reasonably even tempo.

OK, but I do finally arise—gingerly, so as not to waken my chosen one—and I *am* able to move around the room. Outside the window, almost within reach, dangles a grapefruit for breakfast. And there, beyond—the blue-palette special of the day served on the lake, the sensuous pink of sunrise, or rising silky vapors, or the gorgeous, colorless calm of a pond at dawn. Ah, the splendid simplicities. How'd I get this lucky?

Engaged in a grinning brushing of teeth, and a quick rejuvenating shave, I could well ponder about what happened to the kid who once looked back at me from the mirror. Instead, I think of my dad, about whom it was once said "his face is the map of Ireland."

Would anyone say of me, here or on foreign soil, that I bear the map of the U.S.A. on my face?

My eyes have been blessed to see much of this beloved territory, from the 1920s to the 21st century—a favored time and place to have existed.

Why me?

To have *lived* in the age of horse-drawn milk wagons and jet airliners, to have heard music on a crystal set, and watched the Notre Dame–Southern Cal football game on a box in the corner where the radio once stood on four legs.

Yes, and to have eaten food fixed on a wood stove and in a microwave oven. To have learned the Great Depression's lessons of sacrifice, sharing, and love. To have personally known the advent and impact of miracle medicine.

And in my lifetime the "Star-Spangled Banner" became our official National Anthem.

Well, nobody claims it's perfect, the song *or* this land inhabited by flawed males and females, one of whom had it in his heart to assassinate a president.

Go ahead, count the riots, wars, strikes, plagues, terrorism, swindles, the beggars, the homeless. Sure, I know what it's like to be penniless and jobless, but I don't know how it feels that nobody ever cared when or where I'd ever get back on my feet.

I might yelp about escalating taxes and worry about my pension fund holding up, but here's the point. Except for an act of providence, I might be starving in South Africa, or dodging snipers in the Middle East. Has someone failed to add up the sins of my past?

In the kitchen, the morning newspaper in my hands, I wait for the girl of my dreams to come join me.

Thank you, thank you, but why me, oh, Lord?

If you enjoyed reading this book, here are some other Pineapple Press titles you might enjoy as well. To request our complete catalog or to place an order, write to Pineapple Press, P.O. Box 3889, Sarasota, Florida 34230, or call 1-800-PINEAPL (746-3275). Or visit our website at www.pineapplepress.com.

Bansemer's Book of the Southern Shores by Roger Bansemer. This artist's journal describes in words and vibrant images the colorful places nestled up and down the Southern coasts of the U.S. as he strolls through the towns, guides his boat along the white beaches, and chats with the locals. ISBN 1-56164-294-0 (hb)

The Everglades: River of Grass, 50th Anniversary Edition by Marjory Stoneman Douglas. This is the treasured classic of nature writing, first published 50 years ago, that captured attention all over the world and launched the fight to save the Everglades. ISBN 1-56164-135-9 (hb)

Journey to Titanic by Roger Bansemer. Through his stunning artwork and vivid writing, the author relays the colorful characters on an expedition to one of history's most famous shipwrecks, the history and past grandeur of the *Titanic,* and the aching beauty of the ship's underwater remains. ISBN 1-56164-292-4 (hb); 1-56164-293-2 (pb)

Marjory Stoneman Douglas: Voice of the River by Marjory Stoneman Douglas with John Rothchild. Nationally known as the First Lady of Conservation and the woman who "saved" the Everglades, Marjory Stoneman Douglas (1890–1998) founded the Friends of the Everglades. This story of her influential life is told in a unique and spirited voice. ISBN 0-910923-33-7 (hb); ISBN 0-910923-94-9 (pb)

Florida's Past Volumes 1, 2, and 3 by Gene Burnett. Collected essays from Burnett's "Florida's Past" columns in *Florida Trend* magazine, plus some original writings not found elsewhere. Burnett's easygoing style and his sometimes surprising choice of topics make history good reading. Volume 1 ISBN 1-56164-115-4 (pb); Volume 2 ISBN 1-56164-139-1 (pb); Volume 3 ISBN 1-56164-117-0 (pb)

Florida in Poetry edited by Jane Anderson Jones and Maurice O'Sullivan. The first comprehensive anthology of Florida poetry that features a cross-section of voices enchanted by, complaining about, wondering at, and disgusted with Florida's environment and character. Includes poems by Walt Whitman, Langston Hughes, and Elizabeth Bishop, among many others. ISBN 1-56164-083-2 (hb)

The Florida Chronicles by Stuart B. McIver. A series offering true-life sagas of the notable and notorious characters throughout history who have given Florida its distinctive flavor. Volume 1: *Dreamers, Schemers and Scalawags* ISBN 1-56164-155-3 (pb); Volume 2: *Murder in the Tropics* ISBN 1-56164-079-4 (hb); Volume 3: *Touched by the Sun* ISBN 1-56164-206-1 (hb)

The Florida Keys by John Viele. The trials and successes of the Keys pioneers are brought to life in this series, which recounts tales of early pioneer life and life at sea. Volume 1: *A History of the Pioneers* ISBN 1-56164-101-4 (hb); Volume 2: *True Stories of the Perilous Straits* ISBN 1-56164-179-0 (hb); Volume 3: The Wreckers ISBN 1-56164-219-3 (hb)